NETIQUETTE ESSENTIALS
NEW RULES FOR MINDING YOUR MANNERS IN A HIGH-TECH WORLD

By
SCOTT STEINBERG

With
Damon Brown

STRATEGIC CONSULTING | PRODUCT TESTING | MARKET RESEARCH | EXPERT WITNESSES

www.TechSavvyGlobal.com

AS SEEN ON

3

NETIQUETTE ESSENTIALS
NEW RULES FOR MINDING YOUR MANNERS IN A HIGH-TECH WORLD

To order copies or reprints, contact the publisher at:

Published by READ.ME and TechSavvy Global LLC

www.AKeynoteSpeaker.com

www.TechSavvyGlobal.com

DEDICATION

For family and friends, who've watched us break nearly every rule in the book, and for all the businesses, brands and families currently living and working in the age of Generation Tech. A word to the wise: In a world of constant connectivity, there's still something to be said for knowing when to power down.

PREFACE

Watch carefully, and you can see society changing before your very eyes. A woman accidentally walking headfirst into a lamppost because she was too busy texting to look up; a first date getting dumped because they couldn't be bothered to shut off their smartphone during dinner, or were caught posting unwanted updates to Facebook in the middle of dessert; even a co-worker being fired for sending inappropriate instant messages or posting comments critical of their employer on his or her personal blog. Thanks to the advent of new technologies and corresponding forms of communication, these scenarios are, sadly, becoming all too common.

Granted, each of the above examples may be extreme. But they do underscore a growing point of concern for parents, educators and working professionals alike. Specifically: In a world where high-tech ways to communicate continue to grow by leaps and bounds, yet personal communication skills and polished manners are already becoming increasingly rare, how do we determine what's acceptable from the standpoint of everyday courtesy? And, for that matter, how do we delineate formal rules of propriety – let alone observe them – when the tools and technologies we utilize are constantly changing? Given the seismic impact that high-tech solutions and devices have had on our interpersonal dealings, it's become a growingly difficult question to address – and one of paramount importance that we answer.

That's why this book was written: In hopes of equipping contemporary high-tech users with the tools and training they need to not only be courteous and respectful of others, but also responsible digital citizens. And, of course, encouraging all to not only take part in the conversation, but also actively engage in the discussion and debates that will ultimately shape tomorrow's rules of conduct and behavior, to the benefit of future generations. Not only is it becoming increasingly clear that there's a pressing need to provide consumers of high-tech products and services with the skills they need to positively integrate technology into their everyday lives. There's a vital need to do it here and now, before a failure to maintain adequate standards of courtesy within the Internet's permanent and highly visible confines leaves a potentially lasting, pronounced and detrimental mark on their lives and careers.

It's our sincere hope that the thorough guidelines laid out ahead will help teach proper netiquette, and provide you with the essential skills necessary to navigate the high-tech world's constantly shifting roadmap. Our intention is not to lay down iron-clad rules: Rather, simply create an initial foundation and set of parameters that today's growingly tech-savvy communities can contemplate, deliberate and – most importantly – expand and build upon. As the opening statement in what promises to be a long and fascinating discourse, we greatly look forward to hearing your thoughts on what looks to be one of the future's hottest topics, and engaging with millions more as they add their voices to the conversation.

AN INTRODUCTION TO NETIQUETTE

Look down at your phone, look up at your computer, even sit back and study your TV. Virtually every aspect of our lives – and nearly every personal interaction or major household and workplace object contained within them – has been dramatically changed by the advent of technology. If you were just turning 18 today, brick-sized "portable" cell phones, PCs running on dial-up modems and televisions without time-shifting digital video recorders (DVRs) would have been the norm the year you were born. Today, smart-phones offering constant online connectivity, tablet PCs featuring streaming on-demand multimedia, and social networks that instantly connect you with thousands of people worldwide are just a single tap away.

Technology used to tie you down, but now it frees you – or at least appears to do so, at a passing glance. But dig deeper and you'll soon discover the growing challenge that today's modern businesses and families are rapidly becoming all too aware of: For every new opportunity innovative apps, gadgets and software programs introduce, they also present new wrinkles. With Twitter, Facebook and LinkedIn becoming a bigger part of everyday life, Google searches commonplace when researching new hires or prospective college recruits, and the ability to post photos, videos and status updates online on-demand from virtually anywhere growing, consider. With great power comes the responsibility to be increasingly aware of the software and devices we use, how we utilize them, and the way in which our online and high-tech interactions impact others.

Case in point: Nowadays, it's not uncommon to witness twenty-somethings out for an intimate date who will suddenly pause their discussions mid-con-versation and whip out their cell phones to check a new text message. Nor is it rare to spy entire groups of children clustered around the dinner table at a restaurant with their heads buried in an iPhone or portable gaming system. Modern workdays, like the boundaries between jobs and personal time, are also increasingly blurring, given that our mobile devices are many times as powerful as yesterday's computers, and we're literally carrying our business in our pockets. We're not only overwhelmed by the wealth of media options available on TVs, Web browsers, tablets, and through broadband connections – we're increasingly struggling to comfortably incorporate them into our everyday lives and social interactions as well.

As is evident at a glance, these new high-tech problems are most reflected when it comes to modern etiquette and manners. Long a grey area for technology users, especially older generations who didn't grow up with cell phones or portable media players in-hand, even leading experts continue to struggle to keep up, given the pace at which technology advances. For example: Those who didn't grow up with computers in their room, or access to early online networks, may not know that it's awkward, if not outright dangerous, to befriend a pleasant-looking stranger on Facebook. Likewise, contemporary parents may be confused about how long it's proper for kids to spend staring at screens, or when and how it's appropriate to place a cell phone in a child's hands, let alone the actual content and influences which children may ultimately be exposed to by putting connected devices in their eager little paws. Moreover, entire generations coming of age in the wireless era, while better able to juggle its constant media flow and haphazard concentration demands, may be less well-equipped to empathize with others, pick up on body language and emotional cues, or handle face-to-face interactions.

These troubles aren't a passing issue confined solely to tech enthusiasts, either: Over 900 million normal, everyday individuals currently utilize Facebook, 500 million connect via Twitter, and, according to CTIA – The Wireless Organization, there are now more cell phones than people in America. Moreover, the Radicati Group says that at least one out of every five people uses e-mail, and the Pew Institute found that the same amount have read an e-book over the past year. As for texting rates amongst teenagers? Let's just say you'd better brush up on your online slang as much, if not more than, verbal conversation skills if you want to stay in contact going forward. (ROFL) Just one problem: Popular as many of these forms of technology are today, they existed in very different forms two decades ago, if they existed at all. No wonder we're unsure how to handle them!

This is where the following manuscript – a comprehensive guide to "netiquette" (online and high-tech etiquette) – comes in. Designed to answer as many burning questions as possible, from how many hours in front of the PC are too much to the proper way to de-friend former BFFs on Facebook, it aims to decode the rules of high-tech courtesy and behavior for a new generation of parents, kids, businesses and working professionals. An open-ended guide to manners in the age of persistent connectivity, social networks and streaming media, we've also connected with a slew of modern-day tech experts (our generation's equivalent of Ann Landers) to get their inside hints, tips and advice on how to comport yourself in the 21st century.

Note that given the pace at which technology moves, the endless (and endlessly evolving) variety of global and professional cultures that exist, and unique ways in which each individual interacts with high-tech tools, the following rules are merely a conversational starting point. Offering general guidelines and discussion points for experts and enthusiasts to discuss and debate, we hope that they'll provide positive suggestions that can help enhance both your interactions with others and the way in which you interface with technology itself. Only through ongoing and evolving dialogue between educators, employers, lawmakers and everyday individuals alike can we hope to truly define formal rules of online or high-tech conduct and digital citizenship. But in the interests of providing a starting guidepost to navigating the increasingly complex web of high-tech gadgets and services, and growingly sophisticated range of interactions and communications surrounding them, we hope you'll find it a welcome introduction.

For parents and educators, we aim to help you better understand technology and, most importantly, guide your child through this increasingly complicated period. For modern professionals, we hope to demonstrate the best way to maintain professionalism and integrity on your chosen career path, and avoid the many unexpected but often arresting faux pas that could unexpectedly halt your journey. For businesses, organizations and employers, we seek to set initial guidelines that will allow you to create a positive, safe, and enriching environment for your employees. And for kids, whose lives will most be shaped by technology's evolving advancements, we look to fill in the blanks, answer common questions, and equip you with the essential real-world skills, manners and knowledge of protocol that you will need to navigate tomorrow's ever-changing personal and professional worlds while respecting your growing high-tech savvy.

For purposes of clarity and succinctness, we break the realm of high-tech and online etiquette down into six core topics:

- **Social Networks**
- **Cell Phones, Tablets, Electronics, and Mobile Devices**
- **Email**
- **Blogs, Websites, and Online Newsgroups**
- **Internet and Online Safety**
- **Instant Messaging and Chat Rooms**

Each section will provide the information that you need to know in order to adroitly handle yourself in social, professional and everyday life situations. As an added bonus, we've also sprinkled in interviews and insights with leading etiquette experts, relevant discussion points of interest, and (for all you new-comers) definitions of common tech lingo. Future editions will expand and update upon the subjects contained herein. We invite you to submit your own insights, tips and suggestions at www.AKeynoteSpeaker.com – only with your help and insight can we hope to keep future generations ahead of the curve.

SOCIAL
NETWORKS

Social networks – self-contained online forums where users can share their lives and careers and engage in ongoing dialogue with others in the form of text, photos, videos, comments and other forms of high-tech communication – have grown by leaps and bounds over the past decade. More than a billion people worldwide now regularly turn to social networks to provide friends and strangers alike with snapshots and updates of their daily life and, in turn, see what friends, family, and acquaintances are doing at any given moment.

In fact, it's fair to say that today we're juggling two lives: Real and virtual. Some individuals may even spend more of their time operating in the online world than physical. However you use these networks though, it's worth remembering that they've had a fundamental impact on how we interact with others. Before Facebook and similar sites became ubiquitous, the word "friend" referred to someone with whom we shared positive interactions and interests in real-life face-to-face settings. Today, Oxford Dictionaries' suite of products actually includes the following definition for the term: "A contact on a social networking website." When we call someone a "friend," we now distinguish between a social network acquaintance and an actual friend – in the latter case, someone we've met in real life and may even enjoy a deeper personal connection with.

Key to remember here: A friend on Facebook, Twitter, or other social networks may not be someone we've spent time with in the real world, or know particularly well. But they may not be complete strangers, either – or even someone in-between. This begs the question: What do you share with people you've never connected with in everyday life, know next to nothing about, or perhaps have just exchanged minor items in passing? We all have to be careful sharing intimate, personal and/or private details amongst today's fluid social circle. Doubly so, since more unscrupulous individuals could use personal information against us, or share sensitive data with other people that we wouldn't trust at all.

Another issue that social networks present is the false sense of security they convey – much like the Internet itself. From our perspective, we're staring at a cold, inanimate PC monitor, faceless webcam, or glossy smartphone screen, making it easy to forget that literally billions of people may be staring back. And, for that matter, can conceivably access anything we post online, which may live on via the Internet forever. Even top celebrities, who of all people should know how public their lives are, have made epic mistakes, tweeting offensive jokes, posting risqué photos, and even slandering other people, simply because they didn't remember the number one rule of the Internet: Don't post something you'd be ashamed to share with the public at large.

Also crucial to keep in mind when entering the social networking world, given its high level of visibility and shared nature: One should always avoid discussing topics that act as lightning rods in everyday social situations. Think of your time in the social network realm as similar to that spent at a formal cocktail party: Politics, religion, sex, and other potentially controversial subjects are typically best left off the table. While it is ultimately up to you what you choose to share, and acceptance levels differ by individual audience, realize this maxim: Using a social network automatically means that you are in shared, and oftentimes mixed, company – and what appears to be a safe, cut-and-dried subject to you may seem like a radical, offensive idea to a friend online.

Following is a breakdown of four major networks, including Facebook, Twitter, LinkedIn, and Google+, each with a summary, pros and cons, and insider tips to help make your experiences on them both safe and fulfilling.

Facebook

Enjoyed by hundreds of millions of users, Facebook allows you to share thoughts (in the form of text posts called status updates), pictures, and video with other real-life individuals connected to the service (called friends). Note that while Facebook posts can be limited to certain groups of friends, the majority of interactions are public, and highly visible.

Benefits:

o Free and easy to use, and accessible from many major high-tech devices
o Extremely popular – many people you'll know are on it, and may be amenable to using the service
o Fast and simple sharing of text and multimedia content with others

Challenges:

o Ever-changing set of privacy settings and features, which may prove challenging to keep up with
o Some may find it difficult and time-consuming to share content with specific groups or subsets of friends
o News feeds and notifications can get clogged with app or video game requests, self-promotional notices, and spam

Inside Tips:

o Be careful Liking a negative or controversial status update, as it may alienate friends and, depending on their status, even offend the person who posted it.
o Realize that there may be consequences to linking Twitter to your Facebook account, as it may spam friends' feeds by repeatedly posting throughout the day.
o Add a personal note when you ask to be someone's friend on Facebook explaining who you are and why you want to be friends, unless you happen to know the person well in real life.
o Do not feel obligated to friend someone back,

major blog or site that pretty much everyone checks on a daily basis. If you must share, at least bring something new to the conversation like your opinion or analysis of the topic.

3. Checking in has become very popular online, and the practice has its place. For example: I find it handy to check in at places where I want other people to know I'm there, such as a conference or event. It's also fun to check into places to keep a record of where you have been. Just watch the auto-posts of all those badges on the various social networks. You'd be surprised how many people don't care that you just unlocked a "swarm."

4. Watch what you upload and who you tag. In the end, it's really up to the end user to filter out what they want their followers to see... but use a little good judgment when you're uploading pictures and tagging your

especially individuals you don't know, since that may give them access to personal information about you.
o Adjust your settings so you have control over who posts on your wall, tags you in pictures and – via status updates or other methods – can reveal where you are located.
o Always log or sign out of your Facebook account when done using it – especially on shared devices.

Twitter

Twitter is a social or 'micro-blogging' network that lets you share short statements (called "tweets") in the form of text updates that clock in at 140 characters or less. As with Facebook, you can follow people on Twitter and be followed by others, allowing users to track your activity and status updates. Interesting tweets can also be shared (retweeted) with your own friends and followers.

Benefits:
o Free of charge, offers a handy way to exchange short messages, suitable for brief browsing sessions, and accessible from most major high-tech devices
o Fast way to find out what's trending in the world at large, and share information at record speed
o Lets you quickly connect with and follow the activity of friends and strangers alike

Challenges:
o Even private information can be easily shared by strangers in seconds, and impulse-driven nature may lead to unwise posts
o Spambots, or automated Twitter users, may barrage you with ads or harmful links
o Short nature of messages doesn't lend itself well to deep conversations or conveying emotional nuance, and users may discuss mundane topics or minute details of their day that they wouldn't share in real-life

Inside Tips:

o While you cannot directly retweet tweets from private accounts, it's important to avoid copying and pasting them, too, as private tweets have been made classified for a reason.

o It is not required for you to follow people who have chosen to follow you (although doing so in return can be seen as a polite gesture). However, it is important to acknowledge them when they reply to or retweet one of your public messages.

o Think before you post: Is the item you're planning to share of interest, and relevant to, those who follow you? Readers don't need to know intimate details of what you had for lunch, or every micro-second of your day.

o Be careful not only what you post, but also when posting links to pictures, videos, and websites that may be unsuitable for viewing at home or work.

o As noted in the book Damon Brown's Simple Guide to Twitter, retweeting a post gives the impression that you agree with it, as no additional context is provided – be careful what you inadvertently endorse.

o Given Twitter's constant connectivity and often impulse-driven nature, always pause and reconsider posts before you tweet – once publicly made, statements cannot be taken back.

LinkedIn

Dubbed a professional social network, LinkedIn focuses on connecting you with co-workers, employers, and colleagues. It also allows you to create a virtual resume and tear sheet of testimonials that can be shared with potential employers, and reach out to potential peers and mentors.

Benefits:

o Great way to stay connected with colleagues and/or source testimonials even after a job ends

o Avoids the personal, mundane information plaguing other sites in favor of strictly professional communications

friends. Were you at a super secret dinner club? Maybe your friend doesn't want everyone to know they were there. Was there lots of tequila involved? Maybe those pictures are better shared with a smaller group. Make good use of Facebook's friend lists feature to target your sharing and narrow down the potential exposure.

5. Don't mistakenly share sensitive info. Many people don't realize that photos and tweets can contain geo-tags that can pinpoint your location down to a few feet. If you don't want everyone in the world to know exactly where you are posting from, turn these GPS features off.

o Can connect you to new job opportunities and individuals through mutual introductions

Challenges:
o Users don't always update their profile, so information may not be current, or relevant to present jobs and skill sets
o You may find yourself fielding inappropriate or unwanted requests for connections, introductions, or recommendations from third parties, known or otherwise
o Extended site features and connection options require a paid annual professional membership fee

Inside Tips:
o Use a real-life headshot of yourself as your profile photo, not cartoon avatars, product shots or random images: It's imperative to convey a professional image.
o Only ask for testimonials from people that you've intimately worked with in the past.
o Be honest when providing your online resume, as former and present colleagues are likely on LinkedIn, too. Likewise, multiple copies of one's resume may readily be available online – be careful that these documents don't contradict.
o When attempting to connect with strangers, at a bare minimum, fill out the note section and explain who you are and why you'd like to sync up with them.
o Give connected colleagues a heads-up to confirm their approval before introducing or connecting them to another person in your network.
o Reaching out to pitch contacts via LinkedIn and/or blasting out promotional or news announcements through the service en masse is frowned upon – as a general rule, any such outreach should be made through alternate channels, e.g. direct work email contact.

When Is the Best Time to Connect On LinkedIn?

"I think any time is appropriate to connect on LinkedIn. If you're looking to connect with someone you don't know, but want to get to know professionally, make your agenda known when you first make initial contact. Don't send the generic "I'd like to add you to my network" email, but instead clarify who you are, why you're reaching out and why you think it's important to connect."

-Jeana Lee Tahnk, Tech PR and Marketing Specialist

Google+

Newer than the other social networks, Google+ adopts a similar approach to Facebook, but offers the option to divide friends into circles – unique groups whose access to specific information you can control. Essentially, users can individually segment groups by relation, topic or category (e.g. personal friends, colleagues, golfing buddies, etc.), then comment on statuses and share items amongst specific circles to control the flow of information.

Benefits:
o Easy to post multimedia from all Google services, including YouTube, to your profile and share with friends, and enjoy group chat options
o The +1 system and supporting buttons lets you share interesting items from all across the web
o Friends can be subdivided into private circles (work, school, personal acquaintances, family, etc.) so you can control whom content is shared with

Challenges:
o May be less widely utilized by friends and acquaintances than other social networks mentioned here
o Too easy to unintentionally share private or unwanted information with the wrong circle
o Still working to differentiate itself from rivals, and may be seen as less intuitive for beginners than visually-oriented competitors such as Pinterest

Inside Tips:
o As with Facebook, use caution when approving (giving a +1) to a negative or controversial status update – this may be seen as an endorsement of its contents.
o Carefully craft your circles so you'll share notes only with appropriate parties – this allows you to avoid inadvertently sharing data with unreceptive or inappropriate audiences.
o As of Winter 2012, Google ties your actions together across all its services, so be aware that it now can track your activities from Google+ to YouTube to Google Maps.
o Do not automatically reciprocate adding someone to your social circle until you are sure that you know them or want to be connected to them – and then be careful which circle you add them to.
o For your protection, when not in use, log out of your Google+ account on your phone just as you would on your home or laptop computer.

What's OK to Share?

- Sharing extremely-opinionated viewpoints (e.g. political leanings or thoughts on controversial topics) can be a lightning rod online. Think twice before liking supporting status updates or posting such opinions, which can incite and aggravate others (and live on in perpetuity). If you feel the need to express these opinions, consider confining such communications to exchanges with individual friends, or specific Facebook or Google+ groups. Ultimately though, it's important to remember: If you don't have anything nice to say, perhaps it's best left unsaid.
- Posting embarrassing, revealing or negative photos of yourself should be avoided at all costs. Remember: Images you share may be taken at face value, and/or viewed as representative of your character – not to mention live on forever on the Internet. What seems cute in high school or college may not seem quite so endearing to potential employers.
- Never post photos of others without their express permission.
- Relationship or personal drama is best kept private. If you cannot resist the urge to share, do so sparingly – and in the most vague, unspecific terms possible – for the sake of involved parties, or friends uninterested or unwilling to participate in the situation. No communications should be shared about other individuals and those involved in real-life situations without their advance permission.
- As a rule of thumb, uncomfortable or revealing personal information, i.e. details of your struggles with psychological issues or relatives' fading health, should be shared sparingly, if at all, and – unless acquaintances have indicated that they're comfortable viewing this content – only with others you know in real-life. Note that content shared online may further be available for public viewing, and inadvertently expose you or your family to potential risk and/or embarrassment.
- Never share intimate personal details including birthdates, phone numbers, addresses, schools or hometowns online, to minimize risks of crime, vandalism or identity theft. Never let others know when you'll be away from your home, especially for any given length of time, e.g. while on vacation.
- Avoid posting on social networks unless you have a tight grasp over your privacy settings, and are completely comfortable with the group of online friends that your updates will be shared with.

Tone of Voice and Attitude

- Professionalism is imperative – if you wouldn't say it in a social or work setting, don't say it online, in the most public of forums.

- Politeness and respect are vital: Always be considerate of others, and treat them the way that you'd wish to be treated.
- Avoid bad-mouthing other users as it will negatively impact your image and casual bystanders may judge you based on these actions.
- Maintain a positive tone and attitude: Negativity, complaints and condescending messages often reflect poorly on the poster.
- Bragging and self-aggrandizing statements should be avoided, and making them may cause you to lose friends and followers.
- Since social networks are shared venues enjoyed in mixed company, always avoid using vulgar language and making derogatory remarks.
- Demanding that others share your status updates, projects, thoughts or ideas is inappropriate.
- Reserve confidential discussions for private message threads or, better yet, phone calls, emails or other venues where interactions aren't recorded in perpetuity online.
- Be advised that conversational nuances and subtle shifts in tone or personality may be lost in translation, and that individual users may interpret messages differently: Consider how posts will be read and interpreted before sending.
- Poor spelling, punctuation, grammar and choice of words can reflect equally poorly upon the individual – proofread all communications before sending. Shorthand, abbreviations and online slang should be avoided if possible, and used only in the most informal of conversations.

Being a Responsible User

- Understand that each social network has its own rules of conduct, social norms and methods of interaction. Before utilizing one, take a moment to step back and observe how interactions take place, so you can discern appropriate rules of posting, sharing and behavior.
- Assume that everything you post online can be seen by others, as even major social networks have suffered privacy breaches.
- Do not share information that online friends have shared with you in confidence, i.e. quoting someone's private tweet to you.
- Log out of all your social networks when finished using them, and when you are using a computer or mobile device that isn't yours.
- Realize that everything posted online lives on the Internet permanently, and may be available for public viewing.
- Never forget: Despite their seemingly intimacy, social networks are among

the most public of spaces – it's important to conduct yourself on them as you would in any shared setting.

- You reserve the exclusive right, and it is wholly appropriate, to decline friend requests from strangers.
- Privacy and personal comfort are paramount: At no point should you feel compelled to respond to messages or queries from people you don't know.
- Before posting on others' profiles or walls, or tagging them in your own posts, consider how your actions and/or statements may be perceived, and if they may potentially cast friends in a negative light and/or embarrass them.
- Use privacy settings to limit who can view your posts and shares.
- When asking someone you don't know to be your friend, send a short message explaining who you are and why you're attempting to contact them.
- Sharing extremely-opinionated viewpoints (e.g. political leanings or thoughts on controversial topics) can be a lightning rod online. Think twice before liking supporting status updates or posting such opinions, which can incite and aggravate others (and live on in perpetuity). If you feel the need to express these opinions, consider confining such communications to exchanges with individual friends, or specific Facebook or Google+ groups. Ultimately though, it's important to remember: If you don't have anything nice to say, perhaps it's best left unsaid.
- Posting embarrassing, revealing or negative photos of yourself should be avoided at all costs. Remember: Images you share may be taken at face value, and/or viewed as representative of your character – not to mention live on forever on the Internet. What seems cute in high school or college may not seem quite so endearing to potential employers.
- Never post photos of others without their express permission.
- Relationship or personal drama is best kept private. If you cannot resist the urge to share, do so sparingly – and in the most vague, unspecific terms possible – for the sake of involved parties, or friends uninterested or unwilling to participate in the situation. No communications should be shared about other individuals and those involved in real-life situations without their advance permission.
- As a rule of thumb, uncomfortable or revealing personal information, i.e. details of your struggles with psychological issues or relatives' fading health, should be shared sparingly, if at all, and – unless acquaintances have indicated that they're comfortable viewing this content – only with others you know in real-life. Note that content shared online may further

be available for public viewing, and inadvertently expose you or your family to potential risk and/or embarrassment.

- Never share intimate personal details including birthdates, phone numbers, addresses, schools or hometowns online, to minimize risks of crime, vandalism or identity theft. Never let others know when you'll be away from your home, especially for any given length of time, e.g. while on vacation.
- Avoid posting on social networks unless you have a tight grasp over your privacy settings, and are completely comfortable with the group of online friends that your updates will be shared with.

LIFE

Online Dating and Relationships

- If your real-world relationship status changes, wait to change your Facebook status until after you've cleared it with your significant other.
- Tweeting or posting status updates during a date is always bad, as it shows you're not fully present and focused on the date.
- Quickly reading up on others on Facebook is OK, but be careful how deep you dig – sifting through their entire life history or plowing through all their pictures could fall into stalker territory.
- If you meet someone in real-life circumstances, e.g. at a bar or a party, first continue the conversation over email or the phone before connecting on Facebook and sharing your private information.

Friending and De-Friending Others, Including Real-Life Friends and Family

- Only friend people you would be comfortable sharing the ins-and-outs of your day with in real life.
- It is OK to de-friend any and all individuals whom you don't feel comfortable sharing updates with. Many sites allow you to quietly de-friend individuals without notifying them, or ignore friend requests in perpetuity, while allowing the option for them to continue receiving status updates.
- Parents should always discuss the prospect of adding children to their friends or followers list with their kids prior to making what may be seen as embarrassing and intrusive requests.
- If you're concerned about kids' safety, it's OK to require that your profile be connected to children's profiles as a condition of their usage of social networks. However, it is inappropriate to post on your child's wall or send public (and potentially embarrassing) messages to them.
- If you're not ready to de-friend someone completely on a social network, consider moving them into a

then, before leaving for the day, I would pull that person aside and say to them, "I appreciate your friend request, however I have a lot of personal pictures on my profile from my childhood and adolescence that don't accurately reflect the person that I am today. I'd hate to tarnish my image or reputation within the firm based upon some old photos posted by my close friends or family. I hope you understand."

By nipping it in the bud immediately, the topic is a moot point, and you can go about your business regularly tomorrow, knowing that it is covered. "

lower-profile friend category where you can share less posts with them and receive less information about their lives.

- In many cases, there is no notice sent when you de-friend a person, so they won't know they've been downgraded unless they happen to visit your page and don't see the respective friend icon checked.

When to Log Off

- Always log off after using public computers or high-tech devices.
- Never click the "Remember Me" or "Remember My Password" option when logging into a social network unless you own the device from which it's being accessed, as others may be able to access your social network in your absence.
- Should a user inadvertently leave their login open, under no circumstance is it appropriate to utilize or sift through their personal accounts.

Adding Photos

- Facebook, Twitter, LinkedIn, and Google+ all have policies against profane or violent photos – none of which are appropriate to share.
- A picture is worth a thousand words – make sure they're all positive: As a general rule, only post photos that you would be comfortable sharing with your parents.
- Be careful tagging others in photos, as they may not wish the photo or its contents to be visible to other friends on the site.

Posting to Someone's Wall or Adding Them to Groups

- Think carefully before posting on someone's wall or adding people to groups, and always seek their permission in advance.

SEXY PHOTOS – TO SEND, OR NOT TO SEND?

Some people spice up their love life by planning a romantic dinner or scheduling a weekend getaway for two. Others are a little more daring and let romance bleed over into online life. How does netiquette play into these interludes and appropriate rules of online conduct apply as relate to sending potentially risqué photos and videos? We asked Amelia McDonell-Parry, Editor-in-Chief of relationship advice site The-Frisky.com, how to handle the topic of hot pics.

"If your face is visible, I recommend that you be very comfortable with these images eventually getting out for everyone to see [before sharing]. (Not that chances are necessarily high that others will see them, but I do think that it's best to think worst-case scenario here.) Then cross your fingers. If you really want to send sexy photos, the smart way to do it is to make sure that your face and any identifying features (a third nipple, perhaps, or a particularly adorable birthmark) aren't visible: That way you can deny, deny, deny!"

- Context is everything as well: Be sure to consider the ramifications of making these connections in advance, as some users may be insulted that you think they are interested in certain publicly-visible topics.
- Before you post, reconsider. Posting an inappropriate message or piece of content on someone's wall can get them in trouble with their friends, family, or even their employer. When in doubt, consider sending a private message or email with the link instead.

Commenting on Posts

- Cursing, incendiary and salacious language is inappropriate to post under any circumstance.
- Always avoid being judgmental of others' opinions.
- Realize that certain comments (intimate missives, items relating to personal or family issues, etc.) are best reserved for a phone call, sympathy card, or personal gesture.
- Be advised that commentary may be misconstrued or taken out of context – always consider the way in which you may be perceived.

- Understand that someone is always watching. Even courts of law can now subpoena tweets or Facebook posts. While you may be joking in real-life, even the most sarcastic statements can potentially seem damning when taken out of context – you never know what may come back to haunt you.

WORK

Accessing Social Networks at Work

- Check your employer's work policy, as frequenting certain social networks during on-the-job hours may be inappropriate or even grounds for dismissal.
- While attitudes towards social networks may differ depending on your position, it's safe to assume that spending time on social networks is frowned upon during work hours.
- Your favorite social network app or video game may tell everyone when you're fiddling with it during work hours, so avoid doing it when you should be otherwise professionally occupied.

Connecting to Co-Workers and Bosses

- Before connecting with your boss on social networks, consider if you'd still want to be connected to him or her if they weren't your boss, i.e. if you ever leave the position.
- Prior to requesting or accepting connections from colleagues, think about material you're apt to share – is it appropriate for their consumption?
- Note that connecting with colleagues and supervisors may expose you or they to information and influences that may make either party uncomfortable – be certain to understand the risk you're taking in doing so.
- When posting status updates, photos or videos, or interacting online, let professionalism rule: If it's unsafe to say or share at the office, it's not something you should project online.
- Use caution when connecting with co-workers, as more unscrupulous colleagues could use private information obtained from social networks against you.

Managing Photos and Videos

- Do not tag coworkers without their permission. Likewise, do not tag colleagues in images and videos that may be perceived as unprofessional, inappropriate or controversial, even within private social networks – and, for judgment's sake, always err on the side of extreme caution.
- Set social networks to send you an alert whenever you are tagged in a photo or video, and check such postings immediately to make sure you are comfortable with the content and context contained within.
- While individual preference may differ here, it's best to save yourself some trouble and skip posting content from informal work gatherings, i.e. office party photos or videos from corporate getaways, entirely. Such settings

seldom lend themselves to depictions consistent with one's professional image, and not all may be comfortable with the manner in which they're portrayed in media captured at these events.

What's OK to Post

- Avoid voicing strong political, religious or social views on networks you share with colleagues and bosses. If it's not OK to say at work, it's not OK to post on the Internet.
- Do not post negative, controversial, rude or potentially insulting commentary in online spaces.
- Don't speak ill of others, or publicly deride competitors – there's something to be said for good sportsmanship.
- Keep discussions about office politics off all social networks and online spaces, even those that you consider to be private.
- It is wholly inappropriate to use social networks to air dirty laundry, or speak negatively of former, current or prospective employers or colleagues.

Ways to Keep it Professional

- Respond respectfully to commentary aimed at you, or do not respond at all.
- Decide how you want to use a social network (for work, social, or personal purposes, or some combination thereof) before you join and begin inviting others to it. Let this decision guide the type of content posted and tone of voice you adopt.
- Promote others more than you promote yourself to avoid looking selfish (and build good karma).
- Be supportive of others and treat them with the same care and dignity you'd ask for yourself.

Smart Online Career Building

- Keep all online profile pictures professional and reflective of the same respectful image that you project on the job.
- Separate personal and professional expressions online.
- All online postings and presences may be accessible to recruiters, colleagues, strategic partners or clients: As such, it's essential to post and represent yourself at all times with the utmost integrity and professionalism.

Pitching Through Social Networks

- With rare exceptions, if someone wanted to hear your pitch, you would already have his or her email address – contacting them out of the blue on social networks is inappropriate.
- Under no circumstances should you pitch an idea, product, or job opportunity on someone's public wall or profile.
- Some users provide professional contact information on their public profile – using it may be acceptable in some cases, though reaching out via any personal addresses contained therein (janedoe@gmail.com) is not.

KIDS

When Kids Should Access Social Networks

- Legally, social networks require that children be at least 13 years of age before joining.
- As all children develop and mature at different levels, some parents may opt to let kids utilize them sooner. However, whenever you do decide to let sprouts use social networks, realize: Parents must make a running commitment to monitoring online usage, habits and interactions.
- Time limits should be set around social network usage, as with any form of screen time or online interaction. Rules will vary by household, but experts recommend no more than one to two hours daily (accompanied by an equal amount of time spent with other activities). Note that time may be added or subtracted depending on how well children keep up with schoolwork, perform household chores or exhibit good behavior.
- Once introduced, recognize that there will be virtually no chance of getting kids off social networks. Realize that making the connection may potentially expose children to individuals, interactions and influences viewed as negative or inappropriate by your family, and monitor their online activities accordingly.

Balancing Children's Social Networking with Real-Life Interaction

- Set a limited amount of time during which kids may access social networks per day, just as you would for television, homework, sports, video games or other activities.
- Designate specific times – meals, group activities, shared family time, etc. – when access to social networks, like any other screen time, is denied.
- Social networking with friends from school may be simply an extension of real-life relationships. When kids are on social networks, consider pointing out if

real-life friends are online – and encourage them to connect more in the actual world.

Accessing Your Child's Social Networks

- In the case of younger kids, it may be appropriate for parents to "share" a social network account with them.
- Any monitoring of social network activity should be discussed with children in advance – but this doesn't mean having to tell them when and how you're watching.
- While you are within your rights as a parent to require that your profile be connected to your children's profiles, always avoid publicly posting on your child's wall or sending messages visible to other users, which may prompt annoyance and/or embarrassment.
- With older kids, consider talking with their friends' parents and see if they can provide insight into your child's online habits.
- Certain situations (cyberbullying, harassment, inappropriate behavior, etc.) may prove intense enough to warrant parents' accessing kids' social networks without permission. However, understand that there are consequences to such intrusions, and make certain situations are serious enough to justify taking such measures – doing so can be a major violation of trust, which takes significant time to repair.

Inappropriate Items to Share

- Embarrassing, controversial and/or unflattering photos should not be shared on social networks. If the photo raises even the slightest question in your mind, consider that it's best left unshared – or, at the very least, limited to private sharing between friends.

public]. I'm a firm believer that cell phones should stay on vibrate. There is no reason unless your spouse is in labor or you have a family member in the hospital to have the ringer or ringtone on.

Other social faux pas regarding the cell phone include texting or talking during performances or movies, making calls while on public transit or in crowded places, and playing games or music aloud (without earphones) while others are around.

Any suggestions you can offer for more appropriate commenting when conversing on blogs?

Blog comments are most interesting when they are insightful, but brief compliments are also welcome. No matter how long, blog comments should be interesting and add to the conversation, however. Length doesn't really matter, as long as your comment is interesting.

I've seen comment-ers practically write entire blog posts of their own in the comments section, and I've been com-pletely enthralled. In this case, the reader usually comments on the writer's work and add his or her own thoughts and opinions on the matter.

Meanwhile, I also see a lot of short, con-gratulatory messages posted such as "nice-ly written" and "cool examples," and those are just as welcome, though not as original and definitely not thought-provoking.

From a business standpoint, how do you handle your su-pervisor wanting to be friends on Facebook?

There are three op-tions here: Accept, decline or leave your supervisor in purga-tory. I prefer to either accept or leave people in purgatory, no matter who they are. After all, I feel it's really not my place to "decline" or "reject" a friendship. I am flat-tered when someone is interested enough to "friend" me on Facebook, but I follow the "must have met a

KIDS AND SOCIAL NETWORKS –
ESSENTIAL SAFETY ADVICE

Both kids and parents often hide behind the rela-tive anonymity of the Internet and occasionally post or say things online that they would not in person. However, despite how it may seem at first glance, Internet activity you participate in is not totally anonymous. Before posting anything, kids should ask themselves: "Is this something I would be fine broadcasting to an assembly or having my grand-parents hear?"

Also, do not friend people that you do not know: This is among the most fundamental social network-ing safety tips, and a simple, straightforward way to keep yourself and others safe on the Internet. Remember that everything online has a network effect. If you friend someone that you do not know, that person may be able to see one of your friends' or family members' profiles, depending on your and their privacy settings.

Similarly, do not post pictures or comment about others without their permission. A photo that you think is fun and silly could be very embarrassing to another person. Even if they are not "tagged" in a post or photo, the post is available for all of your net-work connections to see. And remember, everything that's posted on the Internet is permanent.

- Stephen Balkam, CEO of the Family Online Safety Institute (FOSI)

- Rumors, innuendo, name-calling and negative gossip should not be spread on social networks, no matter the circumstances.
- Parents and educators should explain to children that everything done, said, or shared on the Internet cannot be taken back.

- It is appropriate to ask others to remove photos, videos, comments or tags of you from their profile which you don't approve of.

- You reserve the right to delete unwanted postings or comments from your profile that others have made.

- Do not accept friend requests from strangers – doing so allows them to view content you share, and potentially access information about friends, family and acquaintances.

Cyberbullying and Inappropriate Content

- Treat all individuals encountered online with fairness and respect – the same courtesies you show people in real-life should be extended to the virtual realm.

- Cyberbullying isn't just inappropriate – it's also a serious offense. Online bullying can be reported to the social network provider and the bully can be booted off the site, or – in more advanced cases – law enforcement professionals may step in and take action

- Recognize that children can and will find access to inappropriate content: Parents must proactively educate them regarding its dangers, and equip kids to make safe, responsible online decisions. Teaching positive behaviors and healthy computing habits is essential. Similarly, adults should create an open, honest household dialogue with children and encourage them to come forward with questions or concerns should they encounter strange, uncomfortable or disturbing online interactions.

few times [in real-life]" rule before adding people.

When it comes to supervisors, I am happy to add them. "Work" and "life" are not separate entities for me – I live, and while living, I have work, and I have free time. I am an equal-opportunity friend, accepting workmates as well as playmates. I recommend that others think about life in a similar way – it's much more organic. And furthermore, if a supervisor can't accept you for you, including every bit of Facebook information you've amassed over the years, maybe they aren't deserving of your service.

If, however, you do not want to be friends with your supervisor, simply declining their invite will do. You don't have to explain, but if he or she asks, you can just say that you only add close friends to your Facebook account. Or, if purgatory sounds more appealing, just leave your boss waiting for an answer... forever.

CELL PHONES, TABLETS, ELECTRONICS and MOBILE DEVICES

Mobile devices have truly taken off over the past few years. The popular Apple iPad brought portable, powerful computing to the forefront of public consciousness, and Amazon is now selling more Kindle e-books than paper- or hardback volumes. Amazingly, in 2011, CTIA found that there were now more cell phones (about 328 million) than people (about 315 million) in the US! Alone, the average smartphone, which includes a digital camera and wire- less broadband connectivity, allows you to communicate via the Web, social networks, text messaging and email; store and share photos, audio and video; download and play music, TV shows, movies and games; and access apps, online services and the Internet on-demand. As a result, maintaining proper mobile etiquette is more important than ever.

General Tips

When to Use Phones and Mobile Devices

- Devices should be turned off during meetings, presentations, classes, meals, group activities and conversations. They should also be shut down when entering theaters, restaurants, and religious institutions, or attending person- al and professional functions. As a rule of thumb, devices should be put away and silenced at any time they might disturb others, i.e. when in shared company.
- If you must keep your phone on because you're expecting an important message or communication, silence it or set the ringer to vibrate. Under optimal scenarios, calls will be forwarded to voicemail, where you can listen and respond to them later.
- If you cannot avoid having to take a call or text, politely excuse yourself from the scenario or discussion, as you would when going to the bathroom.
- Whether in public or private spaces, always keep conversation levels to a respectful volume. Shouting into your phone is inappropriate.
- If unavoidable, calls made in public should be kept as short, sweet and quiet as possible, and confined to crowded or noisier areas where less pri- vate space is anticipated.
- Note that should you choose to interrupt exchanges to take calls, the longer you keep other parties waiting, the greater their potential annoyance.
- When speaking in public spaces, avoid sharing private information, as it may be overhead and subsequently shared with others.
- Do not turn phones on during public performances, family gatherings, business meetings, and other shared or intimate moments that could disturb individuals or large groups of people.

- Phones should not be used in enclosed spaces such as stores, subway cars, gyms, restaurants, airplanes, and autos where conversations may intrude upon or annoy others. If you need to make a call, politely excuse yourself and step outside to do so, or wait until you're in a less private or intrusive setting.
- If placed on vibrate, note that phones should be stored in a purse or pocket, so as not to make noise when they shake against a hard surface, e.g. the dinner table, disturbing others with the sound of their vibrations.
- Ringtones may add character to incoming calls, but consider the message they send: Clients may not equate Justin Bieber's falsetto with something they'd expect to hear emanating from the suit pocket of a serious professional.
- Texting or talking on your cell phone while driving may distract you, impair reaction times and endanger others, and should therefore be avoided at all costs. Hands-free wireless Bluetooth headsets may mitigate some issues, but the best solution is to pull over, park and finish conversations before resuming travel.

Everyday Advice and Hints

- Turn off phones' displays when not in use to avoid accidentally dialing contacts.
- Shut down phones and other high-tech devices while in darkened theaters or concert halls, and don't use them during such low-light scenarios – screens may light up and detract from fellow attendees' enjoyment.
- Take caution when choosing contacts to email or dial – an accidental slip of the finger, or gaffe made by built-in auto-correction features, may result in your contacting the wrong party.
- Be courteous and timely about responding to calls, emails and texts – if it takes you longer than 24 hours to get back to the sender, you may want to send a brief note with an ETA when a proper response can be expected. ("Sincerest apologies, I've been busy at work, but I'll do my best to get back to you within the next day or so.")
- Should you accidentally receive a call or text intended for someone else, a simple "sorry, wrong number" will suffice to prevent further communication. Resist the temptation to be rude, snarky or annoyed when responding, and realize that ignoring the missive may result in subsequent attempts at communication.
- Bluetooth wireless earpieces and headsets should always be turned off and taken out when not in use, and are inappropriate to use while conversing

with other. Similarly, they should not be used in enclosed spaces, where they may disturb others. Limited use in high-traffic or noisy public spaces may be acceptable – the same rules for using cell phones, as presented in When to Use Phones and Mobile Devices, apply.

Cameras and Video Cameras

- Do not photograph or record videos of others without their knowledge and permission.
- Do not take pictures or videos that would offend or embarrass subjects.
- Do not share and post snapshots or film clips of others without their approval.
- Do not use cameras and camcorders in private or intimate spaces including bathrooms, showers, locker rooms, dressing rooms or other spaces where doing so may violate personal privacy and/or the law.
- Do not use cameras and video cameras in houses of worship, during intimate personal or family occasions, or in group or shared settings that may jeopardize others' privacy (i.e. wherever the expectation of privacy is enjoyed) or the privacy of their children (ex: your local daycare).

Texting and Messaging

- When abbreviating messages, show knowledge and respect of how the other party may interpret these communications – texts sent to your grand-mother should look differently than texts sent to a teen, as each will com-prehend and react to messages differently.
- Avoid texting private, embarrassing, intimate or confidential details, as these messages aren't just inappropriate to send – they're also all too easy to for-ward on and into the hands of unwanted parties.
- Note that slang, jargon, grammatical errors, and misspellings may save time and give messages a hint of character, but may reflect poorly upon you or send the wrong message about your personal communication skills.
- As with emails or any form of written high-tech communication, note that tone or intention may be hard to convey through texting, and messages may be perceived incorrectly or taken out of context. Consider before sending if the information is best conveyed with a phone call, short note or alter-nate form of communication.
- Double check names and numbers before texting, especially if making a confidential, controversial or risqué statement, lest you risk accidentally reach out to the wrong party.

- Show courtesy for others' time, patience and phone bill by switching from group texts to reaching out to individuals via direct texts when the conversation becomes irrelevant to others, and ask that they reciprocate.
- Don't send others text messages without asking first – not all subscribe to ongoing texting plans, and recipients may incur billing charges as a result.
- Text messaging is strictly casual in nature, and inappropriate for weightier or more meaningful communications. For more important news or interactions (ending a relationship, sharing unfortunate events, etc.) a phone call or in-person exchange is more appropriate.
- Texts should be kept brief – if you need to say more than can be fit into a few lines, write an email or pick up the phone instead.
- Be respectful of others and don't carpet bomb them with texts – before sending, consider if they really need to receive your commentary in parts, or a smiley face separate from the main body of the message.
- When texting people for the first time, or those who don't have your name and number in their contacts listing or address books, be certain to introduce yourself and/or remind them of where you met. ("Hi, this is Scott, the netiquette guy. For our chat at 11A about corporate training services, where would you like to connect?")
- Sexting – the practice of sending sexually explicit material, including nude photos or lascivious references – is unacceptable and inappropriate under any circumstance. A major high-tech breach of conduct, it may also lead to embarrassment or prosecution.

Borrowing a Device

- Do not use someone's high-tech device without permission.
- If they have forgotten to do so, log them out of any social network, instant messenger, app or software program before you use it yourself.
- Getting permission to use a device does not give you the permission to snoop through other people's personal files, accounts, software or media.
- Under no circumstance is it acceptable to read open emails that others have created, or look through their inboxes or sent messages.
- Avoid visiting any risqué, controversial, or potentially harmful (i.e. spam or fraudulent) websites while on another's device.
- Ask permission before changing any device settings – even something as simple as WiFi connection point access – and restore everything back to the previous settings before returning the device.
- Do not change the lending party's home page, or delete or install new software, without their express permission. If you are finished using installed

software, uninstall it before returning possession of the device to the lender.

- Try not to borrow someone's device if you're nursing a cold, flu or other potential health condition that could spread germs and sickness. If you must do so, observe appropriate health precautions (using hand sanitizer, turning away to cough, wiping down the device with a disinfecting cloth, etc.) before, during and after usage.
- Do not delete files or close open programs, windows and documents without others' permission. If you find closing a document to be unavoidable, be sure to save a version (e.g. "save as," not just "save," in the latter case potentially overwriting important data) before doing so.
- Clean up after yourself: If you have disturbed any items on someone's desk, or used up supplies, be sure to pick up after yourself and replace missing items before handing access back over.

Sharing a Device

- Consider scheduling set times during which each user is allowed to use the device uninterrupted, and sticking to those times, to minimize conflict.
- Be respectful of others' needs, and prioritize usage based on sensibility. If someone must perform an important task (doing homework, filing a work report, etc.) it should take precedence over social calls, playing games or enjoying more leisurely or less time-sensitive pursuits.
- Do not open or look through others' documents, files or multimedia without permission.
- Do not close others' open windows, programs, apps or documents without first checking with them.
- Do not save files to folders designated for others' private use.
- Do not delete others' files, programs or contacts without receiving their permission.
- If you must close a document or program, save a version (e.g. "save as," not just "save," in the latter case potentially overwriting important data) and/or save open tabs and files before doing so.
- Log other users out of any social network, app or software program before you use it yourself.
- Do not visit risqué, controversial, or potentially harmful (i.e. spam or fraudulent) websites without first requesting other sharers' permission.
- Make others aware before changing any device settings or making permanent adjustments that may affect their computing experience.
- Do not change the lending party's home page, or delete or install new soft-

ware, without their express permission. If you are finished using installed software, uninstall it before returning possession of the device to the lender.
- Healthiness and cleanliness are essential: The same rules contained under Borrowing a Device apply here.

Video Chat, Video Calls and Videoconferencing

- Dress appropriately for chats and maintain corresponding standards of personal cleanliness and hygiene – your appearance should be both presentable and respectful.
- Refrain from foul language, abusive statements and negative commentary – comport yourself as you would in any polite, real-world face-to-face interaction.
- Clean up surrounding areas and backgrounds, as they will be visible on-camera. Be aware of any sensitive personal information, e.g. your home address, that may unintentionally be revealed during recording by background objects that are visible in the frame.
- Understand that while conversations may be casual, ramifications can be serious – watch what you say and do, as it's all too easy to record and share even what appear to be private conversations.
- Carry yourself as if all interactions were occurring in a public space – you never know who is watching.

Breaking Negative High-Tech Habits

- If you must check your phone, tablet or mobile device regularly, decide on regular intervals at which this task will be performed (say, every half hour or hour) as opposed to obsessively checking the device every ten seconds.
- Be aware of certain activities that do not require your device to be turned on, or during which usage is discouraged, and enjoy being disconnected for that moment.
- Schedule at least one day a month where you do not turn on your devices or, at the very least, leave them off for the majority of the day.
- Set off-hours or specific times of day (breakfast, dinner, during shared family time, etc.) during which use is prohibited.
- Avoid interrupting interactions with others to send texts, make calls or reference mobile devices.
- Turn away from the computer or cell phone when others address you, and maintain ongoing attention and eye contact during conversations.

- While multiple screens may be in use during shared time (e.g. your wife may be surfing the Web on her iPad while you watch the TV), always put devices down, make direct eye contact and maintain attention when spoken to or interacting with other parties.
- Devices should never intrude upon others' space or impair their enjoyment of their surroundings. Ex: It is inappropriate to interrupt the family's TV viewing time with Words with Friends' constant buzzing notifications, which occur every time that the game demands attention.
- Experts recommend shutting off all devices a minimum of one hour prior to bedtime in order to improve chances of enjoying restful sleep.

5 HIGH-TECH ETIQUETTE RULES TO LIVE BY

We asked Rich DeMuro (www.facebook.com/richontech), tech reporter for KTLA-TV Los Angeles and Tribune Television to share his list of essential technology dos and don'ts when using high-tech devices in public. Following are five rules that he highly recommends that today's technology user abide by:

1. Don't put your phone on the restaurant table if you are having a meal with someone important – and by important, I'm talking everyone from the guy you want to get a job from to your mom when she comes in town. Putting your phone on the table signals [the other party, saying] "I'm waiting for something more important to come along." Roughly 99.9% of all texts, calls and emails can wait an hour until you're done with your meal. If you really need to stay in touch, put your phone on vibrate in your pocket.

2. If you do get a phone call in a place where you are in others' company, excuse yourself from the group before talking.

3. If you're in close quarters, don't talk as loudly as you would as if you were in your office with the door closed. As interesting as it might seem for others to hear a one-sided conversation, it's just kind of annoying.

4. Do us all a favor and keep your phone on vibrate in the most public places, i.e. churches, movie theaters and coffee houses. As someone who is in the TV business and routinely in and out of studios all day, I keep my phone on silent/vibrate all day long, and I have yet to miss a huge call.

5. Speaking of movie theaters, it's OK to look at your phone during the previews – but it is not OK to do so during the movie itself. Just lighting up the screen is distracting to those around you.

LIFE

Using Mobile Phones, Computers and Devices

- During dates and other intimate or meaningful one-on-one, group or family events, turn your cell phone/mobile devices off.
- During shared or intimate occasions, your mobile device should be on only if you are expecting an urgent call or message – and if so, set to silent, voice message or vibrate.
- When in doubt, always respect the policy of the event, venue, host or establishment regarding cell phone and high-tech usage.
- Be cognizant of your voice level, as people tend to talk louder on cell phones, and how it may disturb others.
- Publicly using your phone to call, text or send social network updates should always be considered in context: Doing so in the middle of a shared or intimate public space, e.g. a crowded theater or house of worship, can be highly offensive.
- When using a PC in public, consider installing a privacy screen to keep bystanders from observing your activities. At no time is it appropriate to peep over others' shoulder to see what they're doing on their devices.
- Guidelines for use of multiple screens differ by household and scenario – be respectful and observe the rules of your host or home. Whereas some friends and families won't mind you checking Facebook while watching movies in the living room, others may be offended when spouses or children suddenly whip out a device and start doing so in the middle of action scenes.
- High-tech devices should not be used during meals – put cell phones, gaming systems, and other gadgets away at the dinner table.
- Put gadgets and high-tech accessories away when not in use: Leaving a pair of headphones dangling from your neck while strolling about or chatting while holding a smartphone should be avoided.
- While it may be tempting to tap into unsecured WiFi networks, be advised that information shared over them can be seen by others, and usage is appropriate only if access is knowingly and willingly shared by their owners.
- Consider using a headset if you have to conduct phone conversations in public spaces, so your caller's voice won't disturb others.
- Don't ask to use other people's headsets and, if you have to use them, wipe them down before giving them back.

Phone Etiquette with Milestones

- Asking someone out on a date is perfectly acceptable via your phone. However, higher-commitment requests like marriage (or divorce!) should be made in person.

- Texting can be foolish and wasteful compared to having a brief phone call, and lead to less meaningful moments or unintentional miscommunication: Always consider if a more personal interaction makes better sense.
- Communications should be returned in kind: A phone call should be responded to with a phone call, an email sent in response to an email, etc. Texting should only be utilized if a short, simple answer is appropriate and/or required.
- Consider other people's texting plans before sending them a note – it may cost them to receive the message if they exceed service limits or pay by the text.

PHONE FOLLIES – HOW NOT TO USE YOUR CELL PHONE

Daniel Sieberg, author of The Digital Diet, shares one of the most awkward things you can do with your phone in public:

"In my book I call these types of gaffes "tech turds." One of the most damning is just dumping your smartphone on the table during a social occasion. Perhaps when smartphones first became popular the act of doing so was almost a novelty. Now it's just plain rude. It's like you've invited a guest to the meal whose only role is to interrupt the conversation. If you MUST have your smartphone out, then make reference to it and tell your fellow seat mates that you'll only check it if the one urgent message or call comes in, otherwise you have their complete attention. Another game that works is getting everyone to put their smartphones in a pile in the center of the table. The first one who has to pick it up during the meal picks up the check."

High-Tech Travel Tips

- Turn the volume down on portable media and music players so as not to disturb others, and allow for situational awareness, so you can hear honking horns or others attempting to initiate conversation. Note that loud noises may leak from headphones and earphones if volume levels aren't sufficiently low.

- When viewing media in shared company or public spaces (i.e. on airplanes or subway cars), be aware of who's around you and may, accidentally or otherwise, be able to observe this content. At no time is it appropriate to view material that bears a rating above PG-13 in such contexts, or a G rating if young children are present.
- Maintain situational awareness when in motion. At no time should you be so transfixed by a screen that you cannot safely navigate. Staring at a screen while walking isn't just rude – it's also potentially dangerous to yourself and others, and can result in unexpected stumbles, collisions or even serious injury.
- Pay attention to screen brightness. Before turning on devices with light-up displays (i.e. smartphones and tablets) in darkened public environs such as dimly-lit airplane interiors, politely ask those situated nearby if doing so will disturb them. When utilizing these electronics, consider lowering default screen brightness levels to minimize potential disturbances, which also causes them to consume less power and extends battery life as well.

ONLINE GAMBLING: PLAYING IT SAFE

Professional poker and online casino gambling have turned into a multi-billion dollar business. However, this money is still being spent by real-life individuals, who must comport themselves while interacting with one another with the same level of dignity that they would in any real-world gambling venue. Unlike face-to-face competitions, it can be easy to forget when staring at a computer screen that there is a flesh-and-blood opponent on the other side. As we all have feelings, and both emotions and stakes can run high, there are several points of etiquette to keep in mind before rolling the dice.

- Participation in online games is legal, but playing for real-world money is illegal in many countries, even in games of skill – be aware of any laws you may be breaking before taking part in gambling activities.
- Note that in the case of countries where gambling is legal, winnings may be taxable and required to be reported by law.
- Due to issues with legality, sites which offer online gambling activities may be unsafe or unsecured: Before joining them, consider potential security risks and drawbacks.
- If you opt to participate in illegal gambling, you will have

little to no financial recourse should you lose money, fairly or not.

• At no point should you bet more than you can afford to lose – respect household budgets, and understand the impositions that betting more than you can afford to lose may place on others.

• Within online card and/or casino games, tables are usually divided by skill level (novice, intermediate, and so on) – to maximize enjoyment, stay within your designated experience range to avoid the negative experiences of finding yourself outmatched or making novice mistakes that can ruin other people's fun.

• Be respectful of pacing and time limits, as other players may not appreciate you casually taking minutes to make a move while they sit their casually twiddling their thumbs.

• Every online casino's spin on games (even seemingly familiar ones), standards of behavior, privacy policy, and rules for handling disagreements, conflicts or customer service issues can be different – be sure to read and familiarize yourself with the house rules before playing.

• Avoid creating private instant messenger conversations with other players and use services' built-in chat systems to keep things fair and aboveboard.

• Do not place unofficial bets outside of the official website using PayPal or your credit card.

• Be a good sport: Keep interactions polite and conversational. Be a gracious loser, even if the game doesn't go your way.

WORK

Using Devices During Meetings

- Turn devices off during meetings unless you are expecting a time-sensitive email or call.
- If you must take a call or receive a text during a meeting, be polite and let the organizer know in advance. Setting devices to vibrate will also prevent you from disturbing others.
- Should you need to take an important call, politely excuse yourself (if possible) and step out of the meeting room to conduct it, and keep volume levels low so as not to disturb those still present within.
- Texting, sending emails and checking messages should happen only after meetings are finished, or during official breaks.
- At no time during meetings should devices be used for personal purposes, i.e. updating social networks.
- Consider keeping an alternative voice message on hand letting callers know that you're in a meeting and switching to it while you are occupied, so they don't feel that they've been left hanging.
- If you must use an app during a meeting, set your device to Airplane Mode so it won't accept any outside calls or disturbances, and turn sound effects and volume levels to off.

Appropriate Ringer Settings

- Always turn your phone's ringer off when in a meeting.
- When a ringer is on vibrate, keep your phone in your hand or pocket to avoid disturbing others with table shakes.
- Depending on the model of cell phone that you own, your device may also offer the option to briefly flash to signal incoming calls instead of making potentially more disturbing vibrations or rings – a feature that may be worth using.

When to Shut Devices Off

- If you have a phone specifically utilized for work purposes, turn it off and put it away at the end of the workday if possible.
- Do not bring your work phone to family occasions, dates and other intimate or shared group events without warning friends and family in advance, and/or sharing your reasoning, before it becomes a potential annoyance with the host and other guests, whom it may disturb.
- Turn your phone off if someone specifically requests that you do so, no questions asked.

- Be aware of any automated alarms you've set, as some devices may allow them to go off even when they are powered down, or set to vibrate.

Appropriate Interactions

- Employers may have the right to track or listen to messages on work devices, so keep personal exchanges off of them.
- Employers reserve the right to reclaim any devices when you leave the organization, so back up all
personal data (and only personal data) that is rightfully yours and transfer it elsewhere prior to surrendering possession.
- When using shared devices such as fax machines and copiers, it is appropriate to only look at the cover sheet and name – not the actual contents of the transmission, which should be promptly handed over to the appropriate recipient.

KIDS

Using Mobile Devices During the School Day

- Unless used in conjunction with the curriculum, mobile devices should be turned off during school hours.
- Portable devices should not be used to research topics or find answers during a closed test or competitive situation.
- Be advised that facts and information presented online may be untrue or unverified.
- Always respect educators' rules and school policies for cell phone and mobile device usage – failure to do so many result in disciplinary action.

When it's OK to Give Kids a Cell Phone

- Give a child a cell phone only when they will be outside of easily accessible contact and the need to maintain communication is imperative.
- Consider buying a cell phone that dials only your contact number if and when kids need to use it.
- Prepaid cell phones can also let you limit call times and features, and monitor overall usage.
- You may want to opt out of texting plans, and choose a basic feature phone that foregoes bells and whistles such as downloadable apps and GPS tracking to limit children's online interactions.
- Read the manual, research the device, and know the ins and outs of the cell phone you're considering for your child before you give it to him or her.
- Some parents may choose to start by restricting kids' cell phone use to only times when they or other approved adults are present, until children are mature enough to handle calls, texts, and online interactions on their own.
- Activating devices' built-in parental controls settings, which can be password-protected, may help you limit access to the Web, online spending, downloadable apps, location tracking and other features as well.
- Research and go hands-on with any and all apps

VIDEO GAMES AND ONLINE GAMING

Video games, virtual worlds and online multiplayer connectivity used to conjure up images of sweaty nerds atrophying in their mom's basement. But today, thanks to the success of gaming platforms like Facebook, the iPhone, and Web browsers, all of which play host to thousands of digital diversions (many of which are downloadable free on-demand), nearly everyone has become a gamer.

According to the Entertainment Software Association, in fact, the average game player is 37 years old, more adult women play than teenage boys, and the average game purchaser is actually 41 years old. Professional gaming – the practice of participating in sponsored challenge circuits in which players compete in popular racing, shooting, strategy or fighting games, similar to the way professional athletes do in national sports leagues – is also blossoming online. And from massively multiplayer online (MMO) universes, which exist and evolve online 24/7, to casual games that appeal to every age, skill and interest, all are growing in popularity with men and women alike. However, in many cases – especially titles that involve head-to-head online showdowns – it can be easy to forget that we're competing against others, and that there is a flesh-and-blood opponent on the other side.

While motion-controlled titles and family-friendly outings are gaining in popularity, it bears remembering: Traditional gamers and those with an eye for hardcore outings like first-person shooters and sci-fi adventures haven't gone away. However, we now commonly see them mixing it up with soccer moms, grandparents, and other players not seen since the glory days of Atari's arcade empire. Following are some thoughts on how we can all play nicely together.

• Portable gaming systems such as the Nintendo 3DS or PlayStation Vita, and high-tech devices (including smartphones and tablet PCs) should not be used during meals or shared

before allowing them to be installed and operational on phones – some new offerings allow the sharing of multimedia and location details, and access to personal information or private/public communications.

Teaching Kids Positive Computing Habits

• It is inappropriate to be texting, typing, playing games, or using a high-tech device when conversing with others. Full attention should be given to other people when multiple parties are present in real-life. When speaking, maintain direct eye contact, and be aware of body language (sighing, rolling your eyes, playing with your hair, etc.) that may convey impatience or disinterest. Remember: People are more important, and deserve your undivided attention more than, high-tech gadgets, games or software programs.

• Turn ringers off in public places and set devices to vibrate. High-tech device usage is inappropriate at social functions and events, especially those related to family, religion, school or shared activities (e.g. in a darkened movie theater) where using these gadgets may disturb others.

• If you need to take a call or text in shared company, politely excuse yourself to do so (as you would when using the bathroom), maintain low speaking volumes and keep the activity as brief as possible. The longer you are away, the more it may annoy others.

• Read all emails, instant messages and social network posts twice – and consider how they may be perceived – before hitting send. It's best to stop and think before you immediately post or respond: Doubly so if you are angry or upset. Taking time to calm yourself allows for better communication, allows you to rethink contents before sending, and may ultimately save you a world of trouble in the end.

• Assume that any and all online postings (social network updates, blog posts, photos you've shared, etc.)

are publicly viewable and will exist on the Internet forever – and behave accordingly.

- Do not take pictures and videos of others, or share content featuring them online, without their advance permission.
- Treat others with respect and dignity in all online communications, and refrain from swearing, unfairly criticizing others, or making negative, misleading and provoking statements.
- Keep private discussions, details and topics private, and do not share this information publicly online or forward it to other parties.
- Use social network privacy settings to restrict who can see photos, videos, comments, groups and status updates – otherwise, this information may be available to strangers.
- Put high-tech devices away when not in use, including headphones, and be respectful of volume, sound effects or other distractions they may present to others around when utilized.

Knowing When Children Need to Power Down

- Create natural boundaries for technology, i.e. prohibiting devices' use during dinner or at family functions, to encourage social interaction and reinforce that kids do not need to be connected 24/7.
- Turn off computers, televisions, and other screens at least an hour before bedtime to make sure your child powers down before resting.
- The American Academy of Pediatrics recommends no screen time for children under 2 years of age, and that those older than 2 enjoy no more than 1 to 2 hours a day of screen time total.
- Other experts recommend that children spend as much, or double, the same time spent with high-tech devices involved in other activities.
- Some parents require that screen time be earned by doing schoolwork or performing chores, reinforcing that it's a privilege, not inalienable right. Others choose a base daily limit, then add or subtract time as reward or

family occasions. Be aware that they also offer Internet access, and – in some cases – the ability to share virtual notes, chat online or download social networking and location-sharing apps.
- Put devices away when not in use – no matter how much you're waiting to take your turn on the latest strategy game, it is inappropriate to leave your iPhone lying out on the table.
- Good sportsmanship pays: Be a fair player, and kind and gracious to others, even when you're on the losing team. Similarly, it's important to be appropriately humble when among the winners.
- Treat others with dignity and respect, and be courteous in all communications. Think twice before you say, post or take in-game actions that may offend others or detract from their enjoyment.
- Do not purposefully set out to antagonize, annoy or take advantage of other players.
- If other players request help, be kind and respectful when coming to their aid. In competitive situations, do not seek to capitalize on their inexperience with the game, or lack of skill.
- Though it can be a handy way to boost your score, do not single weaker players out and repeatedly make them a target for purposes of personal gain

at their expense. Note that in some highly competitive games, however, survival of the fittest may be the norm – be advised what you're signing up for.
• In games which allow text, voice or video communication, do not make vulgar statements, gestures or insult others.
• When playing social games on platforms like Facebook, don't pester friends with invites to the game, or updates, without first receiving their permission. One such mention may be appropriate if acquaintances show an active interest in the game or topic.
• Every online game, virtual world and game-related forum asks players to adhere to different rules of conduct and behavior: Be sure you've familiarized yourself with them before getting in the game.
• Avoid overly aggressive trash-talking, which can disturb others, and get you permanently banned off of online video game services.
• Keep communications courteous, and preferably within the bounds of monitored, secure online message boards.
• Never publicly share personal information, contact information or confidential data.
• Be aware of games

punishment depending on children's behavior.

Appropriate Interactions with High-Tech Devices

• Teachers and professionals should not regularly call, email or engage in social networking with kids outside of the school day or curricular assignments, if at all. Direct correspondence should primarily take place from teacher/professional to parent, and then from parent to child.
• Regularly monitor cell phone or device bills so you can track kids' usage, and regulate text, data, and phone calls as you see fit.
• You may want to consider not providing an unlimited texting or calling plan, even if it is cheaper, until your child learns how to stick within reasonable data and call time limits.

- If necessary, ask your child to hand over their cell phone when they return home, or at night before bed, so they won't be tempted to ignore homework and other after-school activities, or engage in late-night texts or calls that interrupt their much-needed sleep cycle.

ONLINE SHORTHAND DICTIONARY: A GLOSSARY OF COMMON TERMS

Abbreviated messages have been a part of our language since the Pony Express, but they've experienced a massive resurgence with the advent of high-tech communications tools like instant messenger programs, texting, and social networks. As with previous generations who sent telegrams, users of modern technology often try to compress as much information into as little space as possible. Some solutions, like Twitter, are actually specifically designed to facilitate the exchange of short messages, while others, like phone-to-phone texting, are limited in length by necessity because transmitting each character literally costs the carrier money.

The most popular messaging services today oftentimes happen to be some of the newest, like Twitter and GroupMe, but the lingo has changed very little from the earliest days of the Internet. Following is a guide to common high-tech slang, shorthand and abbreviations that should help you translate these missives back into common English.

o ABT: About
o Addy: Address
o BBL: Be back later
o BFF: Best friends forever
o BFN/B4N: Bye for now
o BRB: Be right back
o BKA: Better known as
o BTW: By the way
o CYA: See ya
o CYE: Check your email
o FB: Facebook
o FUBAR: F***** up beyond all recognition
o FML: For my loss (something didn't go in your

that tie your video game achievements to your social network news feed to avoid inadvertently pelting your followers with spam.
- Turn your mobile device's sound off in public and, if your game requires lots of screen tapping or physical motion, be aware of the level or noise or distraction you're creating, and how it potential affects others.
- Consider using devices' and operating systems' built-in parental controls features to restrict access to age-appropriate material, online connectivity, in-game purchases and music/video content, and limit the times of day when – and how long – these devices can be accessed.
- Parents may want to place video game systems in shared areas of the home so that they can monitor the games being played, how they're being utilized, the manner in which kids consume them (and how often), and with whom they're interacting online.
- When playing multiplayer games, see them through to the end – don't suddenly drop, disconnect or leave other players hanging because you're fed up with losing. If you must step away from the PC, console or device,

be respectful and let others know (including when you'll return) before disappearing.
• If responsibly asked to shut down a device by a parent, spouse or sibling, comply with the request. Make them aware if there will be any issues, such as additional time needed to reach a predetermined point at which your game can be saved, so as not to lose current progress. Requestors may wish to allow some wiggle room in requests to accommodate players' needs, e.g. a 10- to 15-minute grace period to meet these needs, in order to minimize conflict.
• If sharing a device or game, do not pick up others' saved games where they left off, or delete or overwrite them, without first asking their permission.
• If you encounter questionable, unethical or immoral in-game conduct, report it to the game's operator or supervisors immediately.
• Parents may wish to consider confining online interactions to pre-approved friends lists, allowing you to limit Internet activity to exchanges with only those who've been cleared in advance.
• When playing massively multiplayer online (MMO) games or virtual worlds, avoid unscrupulous individuals, shady offers

favor)
o FTW: For the win! (something went extremely well)
o FYEO: For your eyes only
o G2G: Got to go
o GTFO: Get the f*** out
o GTK: Good to know
o IDK: I don't know
o IMHO: In my humble opinion
o IMO: In my opinion
o J/K: Just kidding
o K: OK
o Kewl: Cool
o L8R: Later (see you)
o LMAO: Laughing my a** off
o LMK: Let me know
o LOL: Laughing out loud
o noob: A newbie, or amateur
o OMG: Oh my gosh
o OTL: Out to lunch
o Pix: Pictures
o ROFL: Rolling on the floor laughing
o RT: (in) Real time
o RTM: Read the manual
o SMH: Shake my head
o Srsly: Seriously?
o STFU: Shut the f*** up
o Thx: Thanks
o TL;DR: Too long; didn't read
o TTYL: Talk to you later
o WIIFM: What's in it for me?
o <3 : Love (a heart)
o :) : Smiley face
o :D : Big grin
o :(: Frown
o :P : Silly (tongue sticking out)
o :o : Surprise or shock

EMAIL

Email is still one of the most popular high-tech ways to communicate despite texting and social networking coming into vogue. An estimated 300 billion emails are sent every day! Despite the huge volume of personal and professional messages sent though, many continue to struggle with basic issues such as sending inappropriate messages, online miscommunications, and buying into common email myths. Still the premier way of communicating for many users, proper email netiquette remains as vital as ever.

<u>General Tips</u>

o Email is a common source of miscommunication, because tone, context and subtle nuances are easily lost in translation. Before sending, consider if your commentary could be misconstrued and/or misinterpreted, and if a simple phone call might be better advised.

o Likewise, truly important or time-sensitive queries may be best addressed via a call, given email's periodic propensity to be delayed or misrouted by touchy servers and spam filters.

o Once written, emails cannot be undone – watch what you say, whom you copy, and always think twice before sending them along.

o Don't write anything in an email that you wouldn't be comfortable saying in person – or in public. Easily forwarded and shared, and/or monitored by employers, inappropriate commentary may come back to haunt you. Professionalism is imperative.

o Unless you get a response, don't assume that emails have been received – Internet issues, inbox filters and even simple misspellings of email addresses may result in communications going awry.

o Be careful (and be careful to double-check recipients) when copying and blind carbon copying: A slip of the keyboard, finger or auto-completing contact form may inadvertently send messages to the wrong party, or result in dozens of parties' contact information accidentally being shared with one another.

o When sending to multiple recipients, consider blind carbon copying for courtesy's sake, or creating groups of users which shield recipients contained in the group from seeing who else has been copied.

o If you're going to add people to the email conversation, let recipients know ("I'm copying John Smith, our head of marketing, here.")

o For courtesy's sake, subject lines should be short, sweet and directly relate to email contents: Misleading or false statements, or needlessly open-ended or misleading questions ("Did you hear about...?") will be poorly received.

o Before marking emails as urgent, tantamount to putting an underscore under your message in someone's inbox, genuinely ask yourself: Will the other party consider the query just as important as I do? If not, they may rush to read something that didn't need urgent prioritizing, and be understandably irritated.

o Before hitting "Reply All" – which sends messages to all individuals copied on an email, not just the sender – consider whether it's important for everyone to receive your response.

o Remember that some things are best left unsaid, and you don't always have to have the last word: Cut down on spam by avoiding pointless responses or sly replies that keep conversations going when they've naturally ended. Ask yourself: Is sending that smiley face to the entire email chain really necessary?

o Courtesy suggests that we be timely about responding to emails – most responses should happen within 24 hours. Should you lack time to respond that soon, it's recommended that you at least send a brief note letting senders know when a proper response will be forthcoming. ("So sorry, I've been tied up at work with a last-minute deadline – I'll drop you a line by the end of this week.")

o When away from your desk for travel or vacations, set an out of office response stating when you'll return, and the conditions under which you may or may not be checking your inbox. ("Thanks for your email. I'm out of office on business until Friday, March 2nd, but will be checking messages periodically. Please be advised that some correspondence may be delayed, but I'll get back to you as soon as possible.")

o Free email services are plentiful, but be aware that some may display ads based on keywords found within your correspondence, or may be perceived as being less acceptable or professional than dedicated website email addresses. Use of services such as Gmail is becoming more common, however, and surrounding attitudes rapidly changing.

o When receiving a suspicious email from a service or provider you use, visit the actual company website and log in to research the issue as opposed to rather than directly clicking on any links contained within the email. Similarly, never dial the numbers contained within suspicious messages, but rather call those directly retrieved from the company's official website.

o If you feel compelled to share sensitive info (never a wise choice), use utmost discretion or, ideally, let others know prior to sharing direct quotes or private conversations with a third party.

o Never give out your email account information, login or password to another party. If you do, request that they inform you as soon as they are finished using it, and then promptly change your password.

o If you need to provide your email for an online contest or in order to sign up for special offers, first create a free "dummy" email that you're OK with sharing, or you run the risk of seeing your inbox peppered with spam.

o Save emoticons (characters such as smiley faces used to denote tone or mood) for casual and informal interactions.

o Can the dirty jokes, photos and videos. If you absolutely, positively feel compelled to share them (and oddly, a surprising number of people do), do those who don't wish to receive them the courtesy of asking before including them on email forwarding lists, and allowing an automatic, easily clicked unsubscribe option.

LIFE

Addressing Subjects

- Dear XXX is largely outdated, and too intimate for casual email communications – a simple "Hello Joe" or "Hi Jane," will suffice in most instances.
- When addressing unknown parties, "To Whom It May Concern" is standard.
- While a professional tone should always be maintained, overly flowery or formal emails may also seem as off-putting as uncomfortably casual missives.

How to Close Emails

- "Love" is a term best reserved for an established significant other, relatives, and close friends, not first dates or casual acquaintances.
- "Sincerely" and "Yours truly" may be commonplace within hand-written letters, but best saved for only serious email communications. You might consider using "Regards" or "Best" as closers instead.
- Automatic signatures are OK, but shouldn't be overly intrusive – a name, job title/business name, address, email address and phone number should provide enough room to get your point across. Anything more is overkill – inspirational quotes and rainbow colors included.

The Best Time to Email

- It is rude to email someone for an event the same day it occurs unless there is an established understanding between you and the person.
- There is nothing inherently wrong with late-night emails, but do be aware that recipient's devices make noises when one is received.
- Note that emails received at odd times – weekends, early AM hours, etc. – may send the proverbial wrong message to the recipient. Ex: Was he or she really thinking of me at 3AM? And better yet – why? Be cognizant of differences between time zones and territories.

What is Appropriate to Email

- Intimate or inappropriate pictures should not be emailed – doubly so, as an email privacy breach or an unscrupulous recipient could let them slip into the wrong hands.
- Break-ups, divorces, marriage proposals, and other intimate occurrences

and milestones should absolutely not be handled via email. The more personal the occasion or communication, the less appropriate it is to be conveyed in any form but in-person.

- Attachments are OK to include, but emails should always include a description or heads-up of what's being attached – especially if contained material may be inappropriate for certain audiences. Note that sending attachments the first time you correspond with someone may be seen as suspicious.
- Never click on unexpected or unsolicited attachments, which may contain viruses, Trojans, malware or other harmful contents.

Tone of Voice

- Writing in capital letters is the virtual equivalent of yelling: SO CONSIDER CUTTING IT OUT, M'KAY?
- Sarcasm, wry humor, and other nuanced styles can easily be misinterpreted over email – cut to the chase, and be straightforward in email communications.
- Grammatical errors, problems with punctuation and spelling issues will reflect poorly in viewers' eyes – always give messages a second pass before hitting Send.
- Along similar lines, be cognizant of the attitude you're portraying and appropriateness of the content being discussed – if you wouldn't feel comfortable stating the contents of the message aloud in public, don't say them in an email either.

Avoiding Miscommunications

- It is OK to follow up crucially important or deadline-oriented emails with a phone call.

IS IT OK TO BREAK UP WITH SOMEONE ONLINE?

We asked Judith Kallos, resident etiquette expert at NetManners. com, how bad it was to break up with someone over text, email, or instant messenger, on a scale of 1 to 10. "A 10! I can't believe that would even be a question that would have to be asked. If you get a Dear John e-mail or IM, consider yourself lucky that you found out what a cad the other person really is." The moral of the story is as follows: Don't be that person.

- Emoticons shouldn't be used often, but they can help convey your meaning if you fear being misunderstood.
- Some email clients allow the use of italics, bold characters or underscoring to emphasize turns of phrase. If unavailable, putting asterisks around important notes (*don't forget to pick me up at 9*) may substitute to designate emphasis or importance in their place.
- Return receipts – notifications that confirm when an email is received and read – may appear overly aggressive, or give recipients the impression that you feel they're untrustworthy. Avoid using wherever possible, except when messages are of the utmost urgency.

and better understand the sender's mindset.

- When composing important or high-stakes emails, write them out, save them as drafts, and then read them aloud later and apply revisions before you hit Send. It's always smart to give crucial messages a second read-through.

Appropriate Emails

- Personal commentary and discussions should take place outside of work hours and work-related inboxes.
- Get a personal email address and utilize it in lieu of using your work email address to handle party invitations, social network interactions, contact with friends and other personal needs.
- When responding to mass emails, unless there's a pressing need to converse with all copied parties, do not use the Reply All option instead of replying directly to the party who sent the message.

Adding Users to Mailing Lists

- Explicitly ask permission before adding someone to your email blasts.
- Keep your frequency of email blasts reasonable – although the definition of "reasonable" differs, a maximum of one outreach attempt a week, or every two weeks, makes a reasonable starting point. Note that sending multiple emails of this nature or repeats of past outreach efforts may annoy and aggravate recipients.
- Make it easy to unsubscribe from email blasts, whether it be via a simple reply email or a one-touch online button or contact form – no more than a single action step should be required.

KIDS

Monitoring your Child's Email

- It may be best to "share" your young child's email so you can help them manage letters, respond wisely to correspondence, and watch out for dangerous spam.
- Some parents may wish to urge children to use email instead of the less-secure and more off-the-cuff direct messages found on social networks, which lend themselves to more immediate, impulsive and highly visible (plus potentially problematic) responses.
- If you come across any concerning emails that involve kids, or include troubling exchanges between them, consider speaking with your child, and/or reaching out to the parents of the child in question (or qualified professionals) to discuss these issues.

Creating Email Boundaries for Kids

- Before sending an email, challenge your child to consider if the conversation may be better handled as a phone call or a face-to-face talk.
- Teach your child not to randomly share their email address with strangers just as they wouldn't share their home address.
- Parents may be able to restrict some email access and exchanges by using the password-protected parental controls settings built into modern high-tech devices.
- When introducing kids to email, you may wish to limit children's interactions to messages to only you or your spouse so you can help them communicate and see how they express themselves online before they connect with others.

BLOGS, WEBSITES AND ONLINE NEWSGROUPS

General Tips

Over the past decade, websites have rapidly begun to supplant office water coolers, newspapers and magazines as the place to share the latest news, opinions and gossip. The speed of today's news cycle and at the rate at which stories proliferate online is part of the equation, but websites also give readers the opportunity to respond quickly, anonymously and in often highly-opinionated fashion. The downside being, of course, that we don't always have the time to fully think through our responses as we did in the days of snail mail and handwritten letters. We may also find ourselves tussling with others online who may or may not share our viewpoints, enjoy the pleasure of harassing others, or simply not have others' best interests at heart. Knowing this, and recognizing that these resources are shared public spaces, observing certain rules of conduct and manners when utilizing blogs, websites and online newsgroups is therefore vital.

Rules of Conduct

- Some websites, newsgroups and blogs touch on popular themes and memes; others are purely personal or promotional spaces. Rules of behavior and engagement vary – it's imperative to reference and respect each site's posting and contribution guidelines before joining the conversation.
- Just as you wouldn't jump into a dialogue with strangers without first observing the discussion to gain a sense of propriety and context, don't dive right into online forums. Before contributing, sit back and study how others act (including actual posts, tone of voice, the way in which users interact, and the reactions these interactions prompt) to understand appropriate social norms and the site's overall rules of behavior.
- Promotional posts and advertisements are inap-

ONLINE JOB SEARCHES AND RESUMES

Job hunting has evolved beyond dropping off paper resumes and checking the newspaper want ads. Today it's about registering for recruitment websites, making email introductions through LinkedIn, and sending virtual resumes bouncing across the web. But how can you trust the website or, for that matter, the person on the other end? There are a few new rules to remember when chasing job opportunities safely and securely.

- Observe the same rules of behavior in online job searches as in real-life – professional conduct, appearances and communications are imperative.

- Proper formalities should be observed when conducting job outreach, and care should be taken to respect the rules of grammar, punctuation and spelling.

- Be especially careful with regard to how communications may be perceived – tone of voice, expressions and subtle nuances can be lost in the translation to text.

• Include your name and contact information in all communications, using respectful signature rules (as referenced in How to Close Emails and Establishing a Respectable Signature). All personal contact numbers and email addresses should be separate from your current job contact information.

• Always review prospective employers' rules for submission to determine exact material sought and how they prefer that it be sent electronically before submitting resumes and cover letters.

• Resumes should include keywords (specific phrases frequently used to denote job titles and descriptions, professional experience, and technical terms when performing computerized or online queries). You can many times find

propriate to post at any time. That said, if it fits within the site's social context, a short mention of something you've worked on or contributed may be appropriate in passing conversation ("Thanks, Sarah – here are some handy resources for keeping kids safe online. If you're interested in high-tech etiquette, you might also want to check out this new guide we've written.") However, it's best to do so in the context of requesting others' feedback, thoughts or opinions – not trying to close a sale.

• Spamming other users is not acceptable under any circumstance.

How to Join a Blog Conversation

• Be polite and respectful of others' thoughts and opinions.
• Do not make rude, false or inappropriate statements, including those specifically intended to incite other users.
• Commentary, ideas and points that you're looking to make should be clearly written and spelled out, and facts concisely presented and appropriately referenced or linked to as needed.
• Proper spelling and grammar should be used when entering posts.
• Read what people have posted carefully before commenting. There are few worse things than misinterpreting or missing something that someone said, or repeating comments already made by another user.
• It's always smart to refer to the original post, or quote from prior commentary being referenced, to make it clear that you have read and comprehended the piece and subsequent discussion points.
• Ask yourself: What can I contribute to the conversation? Then do so. If you can't add relevant information, statements or viewpoints of value, perhaps it's better left unsaid.
• Relevancy matters – stay on-topic for the site and thread, and consider whether the information being

shared is something other individuals would actually be interested in reading.

Being a Responsible Contributor

- Name calling, cursing or being argumentative not only creates ill will, but often makes others discount your opinion.
- Logging in or providing an actual name (not posting anonymously) is encouraged, as attribution implies that you stand behind your statements, and are willing to be held accountable for what you say.
- Stay within the realm of the blog's chosen topic of focus, even if other contributors stray from the subject at-hand.
- Treat other contributors with respect, dignity and consideration, just as you would if you were having a conversation with them at a cocktail party or social event.

Tone of Voice, Rules of Conduct and Posting Frequency

- Posting multiple replies before others can contribute looks odd and amateurish – after posting, give others time to respond before leaving additional comments.
- Follow the style and parameters of the blog and its posters, recognizing that a snarky pop culture website may observe different rules of tone, voice and conduct than a serious medical journal.
- Rather than fire off responses immediately, it's often best to wait to reply to a comment challenging your opinion, in order to offer a more well thought out and appropriate response.
- Most major blogs have a rules of conduct or terms of service page – familiarize yourself with house rules before you begin posting.

these keywords (e.g. "systems administrator" vs. "IT expert") in the job description itself. Making false or misleading statements that misrepresent your experience or skill set is unethical, however.

- Be aware that document formatting may not be preserved through all electronic contact methods, and preview all submissions before sending. While your resume may look natty in your word processor, errors including unwanted line breaks, poor formatting and font troubles may appear when entered into email programs or online contact forms.

- Note that resumes, once sent, may be publicly viewable (including to your current boss) and – if you've custom tailored for multiple submissions – in a multitude of forms.

- All online presences should be professional and reflect an appropriate work image – from personal blogs to social network profiles and photo sharing sites, assume that all will be visible to prospective employers.

• More employers and job recruiters are turning to Google, Bing and other online search engines to research prospective hires – be aware of the results that come up, including potentially damaging or embarrassing contents and links.

• Be advised that job searches conducted on work devices and computers may be visible to your current employer.

Avoiding Self-Promotion

• As a rule, self-aggrandizing or self-promotional posts should generally be avoided. If you intend to do so, any comments made to this effect should be made in third-person ("we" vs. "I"), and must be directly related to the post or discussion thread and in some way provide value to your fellow readers. ("Check out this cool website we just finished, which offers a lot of hints and tips that may help answer your questions about netiquette (sorry, shameless self promotion, we know… ☺.")
• Assume that if people wanted to hear your life story, you would be running the blog, not commenting on it.
• If you create a profile for blog postings, add a one-sentence signature (at most) with a link to your website or brand. Avoiding using a giant logo or shot of your product or brand as a profile photo or companion image.
• Avoid attaching pictures or other bandwidth-hogging multimedia to your blog replies, and do not randomly insert plugs for or links to your products or projects.

How to Be Critical and Insightful, But Not Confrontational

• If you are discussing facts, stick to the facts. Do not post misleading or untrue statements.
• If you are discussing experiences, make it clear that it is your personal experience, not necessarily a universal experience.
• If you are accused of making things up, politely and respectfully provide references and links to relevant topics or supporting data.
• Be to the point, avoiding personal jabs or attacks.
• Always consider how others may interpret your commentary and actions before posting, and wheth-

er it's best to clarify points up-front to avoid possible miscommunication.

Dealing With Argumentative Bullies, Known as "Trolls"

- Trolls assume that you want to win every Internet argument and that you aren't going to walk away from one, even as they post statements intended to provoke and incite. Ignoring them is often the best approach: It's hard to keep the flames stoked if you don't help feed the fire.
- Make site moderators and owners aware of the troll's negative actions, which may be in violation of site policy.
- Consider backing away from the troll and not responding. By doing so, you may potentially defuse conflicts by refusing to provide fuel for the quarrel, which can often lead harassers to tire of arguing with themselves. Likewise, as a result of their ineffectual squabbles, trolls may accidentally reveal their true intentions, be silenced by other commentators tired of their behavior, or even wind up banned or blocked from the site by its moderators.
- Be aware of your own behavior, as you may be tempted to tease or bait an emotional commentator on a blog.

Conduct Within Forums

- Contribute to conversations that are helpful to other people, but aren't always self-serving or related to personal interests.
- Read as many posts on the forum as possible to better understand the culture of the venue before posting or responding yourself.
- Remember that everything posted online is permanent, and will reflect upon you.
- Always be honest and up-front, even if you think no one will find out that you made something up.
- Log in and create a profile on the forum, as this makes you more trustworthy than an anonymous poster.

Maintaining a Professional Image

- Fill out your online profile and details before you begin posting, and be sure it's in keeping with the same image you present on the job – including using a professional photo of yourself as an associated image.
- Keep all postings and profiles respectful and professional – their appearance will be seen as representative of your personal demeanor, character

and conduct.
- Understand that you are representing your company at all times in any public space, even if you are sharing a personal opinion.
- Treat everyone with respect and dignity, as you would in any professional situation.

Contacting People Through Unusual Channels

- Directly reaching out to individuals for personal or work-related matters through a public forum such as blog post or newsgroup response is awkward at best. Whenever possible, look for a public or work-related website of theirs that freely volunteers a contact form or work email address, and use these channels for outreach.
- Do not try to reach potential employers for direct job-related queries through their personal blogs. In certain specific cases, it is, however, acceptable to contact them to discuss posts of theirs you've read, topics they've expressed interest in or other public statements that they've made, provided the context strictly relates to the publicly-viewable item in question. Note that this may lead into a more natural dialogue during which your interest in potential employment may come up. However, such discussion must occur organically – direct outreach via personal spaces regarding immediate purposes of employment or lead generation is a breach of etiquette.
- Access journalists and other professionals only through the channels that they personally designate and assume that if they want to contact you, they will contact you back.

BALANCING TECHNOLOGY AND REAL LIFE

Despite writing a book about high-tech addiction, author Daniel Sieberg isn't necessarily opposed to innovation. In fact, his recent volume The Digital Diet is really about finding a way to better balance technology's impact on your life. Here, he shares a few suggestions for walking the tightrope.

Q: How do you handle getting a text during an intimate moment, like during a date?

A: Do not be sneaky about it! Everyone can tell when you're just sliding your fingers under the table to fire off a quick text. It will impress your date if you make a point of NOT answering the text or call. If you see that a text requires immediate attention, then ask if you can be excused later on in the night to check it. Yes, you could also dash to the bathroom if it's really that dire. Or you could take a deep breath, appreciate that whatever it is can wait, and enjoy the company of the human being sitting in front of you.

Q: To enjoy a healthy life, what is the average number of hours that we should spend on the Internet daily?

A: This is a tricky one. Being "online" isn't what it used to be. Once, it was a finite experience when we logged on and then logged off. Today, thanks to smartphones and WiFi networks, we're practically online all the time. In the book, I do suggest thinking about your "e-day" or when you first dive into the Internet and when you turn everything off (or at least put your devices away). To help with that, try charging your smartphone anywhere except the bedroom. We all know it makes a great alarm clock, but providing yourself a little distance could provide a little sanity in the process. And it probably only takes 30 seconds to get anywhere in your abode to get to your smartphone in the morning. But in the meantime, you could also have some coffee, talk to the person next to you, or even enjoy some exercise. The bottom line is that it may not come down to a specific "number" of hours but the quality of that time and feeling more in control.

Q: How appropriate is it to have multiple cell phones and in what cases is it appropriate?

Engineers or programmers testing different smartphone platforms probably need multiple devices. Some workplaces insist on a personal device and a work one (although that trend is fading). Also if you have four ears and two heads then it's probably acceptable. Consolidate if you can! That's the beauty of smartphones – they can merge everything into one. I used to have a pager, an IM device, a digital camera, a PDA and a paper calendar (yes, I'm that old). Nowadays, that's all contained in a smartphone alongside the power of apps, browsing the web, games, etc. Unless you enjoy the Batman "utility belt" look, then I'd recommend minimizing the smartphones. It will cut down on the cords for recharging, too. And isn't life about untangling the wires?

INTERNET AND ONLINE SAFETY

As modern technology users, we're eager to take to the cloud, sharing our personal and professional data over the Internet. But the risks are plentiful. Nearly 900 million of us share our lives on Facebook, with several million using check-in services like Foursquare and Path to tell people our every move. Meanwhile, we're replacing old-fashioned hard drives with cloud-based storage solutions like Dropbox and YouSendIt.com, putting our precious, valuable, and, in some cases, even intimate information into a virtual vault for safekeeping. It's telling that Facebook, Path, and Dropbox have all suffered major security breaches, reminding us how insecure our secure information really is at any given moment.

Mobile security is crucial to keep in mind, too. According to Javelin Research, nearly one out of every ten smartphone owners was a victim of identity theft in 2011. This was likely because a third of smartphone users didn't update to the latest, most secure software and a whopping two-thirds had no password installed on their phone. Today's cell phones are more powerful than yesterday's computers, and yet we don't always remember the power we have in our hands – and the potential authority that we place in someone else's if these devices are stolen.

Interacting wisely online and being a responsible digital citizen is the last piece to understanding holistic Internet security. According to the Pew Research Center, nearly nine out of every ten kids has witnessed an act of cruelty while on social networks, showing us that we're not even effectively protecting our most vulnerable citizens from inappropriate online content. The problem, of course, is that many adults aren't completely aware of what is appropriate online, whether it is posting controversial content on social networks or connecting with strangers on these same channels faster than they would someone in real life. In this day and age, appropriate online etiquette and conduct not only refers to maintaining proper manners, but being smart with how you protect yourself online as well.

General Tips

Adding Antivirus and Pop-Up Blockers

- It is a myth that smartphones and Mac computers do not get viruses, so make sure that all your mobile devices and systems have the latest anti-virus and anti-spam protection software installed. Many companies offer paid solutions (following free 30-day trials), while others provide completely free alternatives.
- Regularly update programs and operating systems. Take software update notices seriously as they may patch up a security breach in your current software, device or operating system's settings.
- Nearly every modern Web browser has a built-in pop-up blocker to stop spam ads, often found under the Preferences menu.

Preventing Identity Theft and Data Breaches

- Create secure passwords that employ a sequence of numbers, letters, and characters into a code that only you know.
- Do not use the same password on multiple sites.
- If you need to keep a record of your passwords on your PC (not advised), be sure to encrypt the file.
- Avoid odd or unexpected email attachments, as they may contain spam or harmful programs, and have senders give you a heads-up before they send attachments or add-ons.
- Cloud backup solutions are convenient, but be aware that anything uploaded to the Internet may be fair game for third-parties to access should a security breach occur – consider the sensitivity of the data you store remotely.
- Make sure that all software is completely up to date and your virus protection subscription is current.
- If an incoming call or email seems suspicious, hang up or close the email and contact the company directly through the main number or email contained on their official website or other corporate channels. Do not click on any links in suspicious emails, or use phone numbers contained within.

Protecting Yourself from Criminals and Predators

- Assume any opportunities to make money quickly (i.e. get rich quick schemes) are traps. Chances are, you probably don't know an exiled Nigerian prince, or have a rich uncle who's just dying to hand over $1 million.

- Make it a policy to change your online passwords at least once a month, and more frequently if you perform a lot of online transactions.
- If you call for assistance with a website, the help center will rarely, if ever ask for your online password or full personal details – the last four digits of a credit card are more likely. If you're worried of putting your personal credit card at risk, consider using prepaid cards for any online activity.
- Look for odd word choices, suspicious behavior, and other telltale signs of fraudulent activity when you're interacting with a new face online, and consider any oddities shown or strange requests made during conversation.
- Do not connect with strangers through social networks, as it exposes any information shared on them, potentially including valuable details of your everyday life, to someone you don't know.

LIFE

"Being cognizant of the type of websites you're visiting is the first step to staying safe online. Don't access sites that require you compromise confidential information, like online banking accounts, credit card numbers, etc. Visit secure websites and always log-off of sites and close out of them when you're done using them."

- Jeana Lee Tahnk, Tech PR and Marketing Specialist

Secure Online Shopping

• When possible, use trusted online payment services to perform online transactions.
• Consider using a prepaid card or gift card in place of your own credit card when shopping online, and a separate email account from your personal one when registering with merchants. In the latter case, many free services such as Gmail offer immediate solutions.
• Do not make major purchases on any computers or devices other than your own.
• If you aren't comfortable with the website or the computer, call the company directly to make a purchase.
• Never share your credit card numbers or other personal details over instant messenger, text, chat rooms, email, social networks or other forms of online communication.

What Not to Share Online

• Never share information online that you wouldn't give to a stranger, including phone numbers, social security numbers, addresses, hometowns, birthdays and other personal details.
• Use caution with location-based mobile software, including social networks, photo sharing and search apps, which can tell strangers where you are if you don't restrict their privacy settings.
• Many new apps allow you to use your Facebook, Twitter or LinkedIn account to log in, but, if possible, create a separate username/password rather than linking them to core accounts and sharing your private user information.

Health Concerns: Knowing When to Power Down

• Experts recommend no more than one to two hours of screen time a day for kids above age two. It's also recommended that high-tech users of all ages enjoy one or two hours away from screens for every hour spent in front of them.

- To prevent eye strain when using high-tech devices, experts have come up with the 20/20/20 rule: Every 20 minutes, take a look at objects 20 feet away from you for at least 20 seconds.
- While watching a movie on the iPad, using Twitter on your smartphone, and researching information on your PC are three widely different activities, all can create the same amount of eye strain. No matter if you're using devices for leisure, school, or work, all high-tech uses should be considered active computer time when you are factoring in breaks.
- To reinforce good technology habits, schedule one day a month where you aren't actively using devices with screens, then try to increase it to one day every two weeks and, eventually, one day a week.
- Rest your hands at least every hour while performing regular texting or typing to reduce the strain on your hands.
- Create an ergonomic office environment to stave off carpal tunnel syndrome and other potential health issues.

What Is Appropriate to Share Online

- Do not share your social security number online or, if you absolutely must (e.g. in the case of interactions with the government), always provide it to a trusted, live representative over a secure connection where possible rather than over email or via a website.
- Before giving out your billing information and address, make sure you're using a website that provides a secure connection by looking for the word "Secure" or a lock symbol in the corner of your web browser.
- Accurate ages, names and birthdates are required for flights and similarly sensitive or government-regulated services. But in the case of services where they're not legally required, consider opting out or entering false information to avoid needlessly handing out precious personal information.
- Most companies do not need your phone number when registering for services, as often your email address will suffice. Always opt out of providing personal information if it isn't required.
- If you want to get off an email list, nearly every company has a link at the bottom of its newsletter titled "Unsubscribe" that will remove you from mailings.

Protecting Yourself from Creepy Dates

• Get to know people before befriending them on social networks or on any location-based services, whether through phone calls or extensive email conversations.

• Turn off all location-based or location-sharing options on your favorite apps, as even photo sharing, check-in and restaurant search applications can sometimes reveal your whereabouts without you knowing it.

• Change security settings on your social networks, including Facebook and Google+, to block other people from checking you in and inadvertently revealing your whereabouts.

• If you opt to meet a friend from the virtual world in real life, make sure at least one friend or relative knows that you're going to do so, your whereabouts, and, if possible, accompanies you. All meetings should take place in public spaces. In the case of dates, where a third wheel may not be welcome, use your high-tech devices to contact designated watchdogs shortly after the date begins, during any change of venue and when concluded, to let them know that you're safe.

• Even if you think you know someone through your interactions on Facebook, chat rooms or instant messenger conversations, when meeting in real life, still take the same precautions as you would on any blind date.

How to Share Your Email Address Without Being Spammed

• When applying for contests or other promotions that require plugging information into online entry forms, consider creating a "dummy" email address through one of the free email providers.

• If you do receive a company email requesting that you confirm your password, go directly to the company's official website and login to do it securely rather than clicking on a link in the original email.

• If an email looks suspicious, do an online search to see if there are any recent scams related to the company emailing you.

WORK

The Ethics of Employers Asking for Your Online Passwords

- You are not legally required to give your employer passwords to your social networks or personal sites.
- Be careful befriending or connecting with co-workers or supervisors online, as they will be able to access personal thoughts, information, and items shared (or that others have posted about you or on your profile) through your online connection without needing to ask for passwords.
- Should you choose to share your password, ask them to notify you as soon as they're finished utilizing them, and change passwords immediately upon notification. Always change your password immediately after leaving their employment.

Safely Visiting Personal Sites at Work and Vice Versa

- Monitoring and tracking systems are standard for work computers, so use extreme caution when visiting personal, social, leisure or questionable sites while at work.
- Understand that your employer could use your email and web browsing habits (all of which they may be able to legally access and track) at work against you.
- Log out of any personal websites whenever you step away from your work computer, including during lunch and coffee breaks.
- Before you work from home or on a public computer, ask your company if there is any security protocol you need to follow.
- Be aware that any information shared or exchanged over public WiFi networks (such as those available at hotels, airports and coffee shops) may be visible to others.

Ways to Secure Work Computers and Mobile Devices

- Password protect all accounts, software programs and network account logins with unique and not easily guessable (birthdates, anniversaries, etc.) passcodes. Do not share your password with anyone.
- Log out of all personal websites, apps and software programs when finished using them, and close and secure all work-related documents, programs and websites when you are done working.
- Use password-protected flash drives, hard drives or secure online services to minimize the transferal of sensitive work-related data between work and personal emails. Do not share sensitive data over instant messengers or other

solutions that may be subject to security breach. Be advised that anything uploaded to the Internet may potentially be shared and access by others.

- Secure any work-related computers and mobile devices with a password only known by you. Use a combination of letters, numbers and characters, and not one related to common dictionary terms, for stronger password protection.
- Pre-install remote-wiping software to remove any sensitive information when a device is lost or stolen. You may also wish to do the same with device tracking and protection software, which allows you to locate and lock missing devices, sound built-in alarms or shut down devices remotely.
- Shut down computers and devices when not in use.
- Do not leave sensitive documents or data lying out on your desk – especially overnight.

KIDS

How to Teach Kids About Online Safety

- Know what social networks your child is on and keep abreast of privacy, policy, feature, or structural changes so you can make sure ramifications are understood and appropriately responded to.
- Teach your child not to share sensitive information about themselves, family, or friends with anyone online.
- Lead by example: Allow kids to watch as you surf the web or use social networks at home and show them proper online behaviors and positive computing habits.
- Download kid-friendly apps, software, filters and web add-ons that help block inappropriate content.
- Use devices' and operating systems' built-in parental controls features to limit access to devices, the Internet and questionable content.

Cyber-Bullying, Cyber-Baiting and Online Interactions

- As The Modern Parents Guide to Kids and Video Games points out, "instances of cyber-bullying should always be reported to in-game and/or real-world authorities." Inappropriate activities on social networks, websites and online services can be relayed to the service's operator and can get the bully kicked off the site.
- Encourage open dialogue and foster a home environment where kids can feel comfortable sharing their thoughts. Make it clear that your child should tell you (and notify other responsible adults with the ability to remedy the situation) immediately if anything happens online that makes them feel weird or uncomfortable.
- Contributing to websites, social networks, groups, forums or conversations that deride or bully others is unacceptable under any circumstance, and may land you in hot water.
- Teach your own child how to be fair, a good sport, and behave appropriately online to ensure that they're responsible digital citizens.

Appropriate Online Access Based on Age/Maturity

- Thirteen is the age when kids can legally join social networks – but take into account your child's individual maturity, development level and social skills when determining when you feel they're ready to go online.
- Consider surfing the web with your child and, like training wheels, decide

when they understand the strengths and pitfalls of the Internet well enough to set out on their own.

- Place all devices with screens in common areas such as the living room, so you can monitor the content that children are consuming, how/when they're consuming it, who they're interacting with online (and how), and be readily available if they have any questions.
- Experts recommend no more than one to two hours of screen time for children daily. The American Academy of Pediatrics advises no screen time whatsoever for children aged two or younger.

---

3 THINGS EVERY CHILD SHOW KNOW ABOUT ONLINE MANNERS

Stephen Balkam, CEO of the Family Online Safety Institute (FOSI), shares his advice regarding essential rules that parents should teach kids about online conduct:

- Treat people online the same way that you would offline. Comments can be just as hurtful when received on the Internet as in person.

- Not all your time should be spent online. Remember that spending time with friends and family in-person is equally important. However, the Internet does provide great opportunities to maintain friendships with people that may have moved away or can't be see often for other reasons.

- It is important not to get too wrapped up in electronic devices when spending time with others. Family dinners are a good time to take a texting break because your parents and siblings are actually really interested in talking to you about what's going on in your life!

KEEPING KIDS SAFE ONLINE

Internet safety is a big concern for all of us, but particularly so for guardians of kids, tweens, and teens. Few people know this better than Lynette T. Owens, Director of Trend Micro's Internet Safety for Kids & Family program. We asked her for five tips on how you can best protect your child from online threats while still helping them take advantage of modern technology.

1. Be an active participant – I often hear parents say they are surprised about the capability of some technology or Internet service that they've allowed their kids to have or use. This tends to happen when parents aren't fully informed about the technology before they allow their kids to use it. Thankfully, this doesn't always result in any major trouble or risk for their kids, and it can easily be solved by spending a little bit of time using the technology you're going to let your kids use. Whether it's a mobile device, app, or social networking site, parents should give them a try before giving their kids the keys to these powerful technology tools. There's no need to be an expert or heavy user of them, but it's important to have some familiarity with them in order to best guide your kids.

2. Know what you're getting into – Spend time understanding which technologies or online services are right for your kids. Many technology devices are costly, and many online sites are not necessarily designed for kids of all ages. Once you decide what you are comfortable with allowing your kids to use, spend some time using these options yourself before handing them over. You're in the best position to guide your kids if you know how to use the technology personally.

3. Talk to your kids about online privacy and security – Teach your kids to use the strongest privacy settings that allow you to still use a technology or service in the way you would like. Advise them to connect with people they know and be wary of contact from strangers. If someone is offering them something that seems too good to be true or doesn't seem quite right, tell them to trust their instincts and steer clear of the offer or the person offering it. Remind your kids that no matter what they share online, even if it's only with a small group of people they trust, it can still be shared widely by people in that trusted circle. Help them understand how their personal information might be used by an online service/app/website before they agree to provide it, and opt out of sharing it if they have that choice. And always use up-to-date, reputable security software on any Internet-connected device to ensure you and your kids' personal information doesn't end up in a hacker's or identity thief's hands.

4. Teach them to be good online citizens – Remind your kids to always treat others with respect. If they see someone being treated badly online, advise them to tell someone or do something rather than just stand by. Advise them to follow community guidelines on social networks and to respect copyright laws and the original work of others. Remind them that anything they post will be there forever, for a future college recruiter or employer to see.

5. Be a positive role model – You should establish and maintain rules about how, when, and where your kids can use their Internet-connected technology. But lead by example – make sure you act yourself just as you'd expect them to behave.

INSTANT MESSAGING AND CHAT ROOMS

Instant messenger (IM) programs are a great way to talk with other people quickly. Now-standard online vocabulary and shorthand like LOL (laugh out loud) and OMG (oh my gosh!) actually originated with these tools. IM solutions first took off in the '90s with the rise of America Online (AOL), but services such as MSN Messenger, Yahoo!, Google Chat, and even Skype have since become popular in their own right. Granted, instant messaging has lost some steam in recent years, given the rise of social networks and texting options. But the practice still has its place for brief, direct and private conversations.

Consider instant messaging an extension of online chat rooms – multi-person conversations in shared spaces where people can enter or exit venues (sometimes using a password) and join in group discussions. Instant messaging usually consists of one-on-one dialogue between individuals, but in any circumstances – solo or shared – basic rules of social etiquette still apply. Treat conversations made over instant messenger solutions as sincerely and as carefully as you would a face-to-face chat.

General Tips

o When choosing a screen name, select one that's professional, polite and appropriate for viewing in shared company. Be aware that alternating capitals, abbreviations, and combinations of mixed numbers and letters may be perceived as less suitable than simple aliases (e.g. JohnQPublic instead of JqPDude1401).
o Keep interactions with others polite, respectful and professional, and be aware that others may see your communications.
o Do not share sensitive information via an instant messenger, even with trusted associates, as a slip of a finger or security breach could easily expose this data.
o Be cognizant of others' time: Consider whether repeated messages may interrupt and annoy them as they work or go about their daily routine.
o Set your status to Away or Do Not Disturb if you do not wish to be interrupted by incoming messages.
o Remember to change your status when you step away from your device and return, especially since you don't want to give the impression that you're ignoring someone's requests, or take multi-hour lunch breaks.
o Respect people's current IM status: Leave them alone if it says Busy, stop contacting them if it says In a Meeting, and so forth.

o Note that while others' statuses may indicate that they are available, they may not be, having inadvertently stepped away from their device, or become preoccupied with an important work-related task. Do not spam them with messages if you don't get an immediate response.

o Do not send instant messages while engaged in phone or real-world conversations. It is OK, however, to send an occasional IM if directly related to the dialogue – e.g. messaging a colleague to help answer a pressing IT question the person on the phone has presented.

o When exiting or pausing a conversation, be polite and drop a note to the other party to let them know ("have to run – see you later!").

o Use caution when conducting multiple conversations, as typing a response intended for another party, or erroneously cutting and pasting links or snippets of conversation into the wrong window, could cause serious trouble and confusion.

LIFE

Dating and Relationships

- Be careful not to reveal your location, name, phone number or other sensitive personal information to people you do not know yet.
- If you want to share personal details, consider using the phone or meeting in person.
- When meeting strangers in real-life, make sure at least one friend or relative knows that you're going to do so, your whereabouts, and, if possible, accompanies you. All meetings should take place in public spaces. In the case of dates, where a third wheel may not be welcome, use your high-tech devices to notify friends at the beginning of the encounter, during the date (if you change venue), and when you get back home safely.
- Even if you think you know someone through your interactions on instant messenger conversations or chat rooms, when meeting in real life, take the same precautions as you would on any blind date.
- IMing risqué photos isn't just wholly inappropriate – it's less secure than emailing them... and emailing them isn't very secure to begin with. In many cases, it's also a crime.
- Make sure you know whom you are speaking to over IM, even if they appear under the same username/handle, as sometimes people share IM addresses, or others (e.g. mischievous siblings and roommates) may be able to access the account from home or work.
- If uncertain whom you're speaking with, don't be afraid to ask questions that only the person you've been conversing with prior would know.

Avoiding Potential Misunderstandings Over IM

- Like email, IM is usually too limited to have complex, nuanced conversations – save subtleties for direct, more personal forms of communication
- If asking a deep or serious question, give the recipient adequate time to reply before you talk again.
- Keep in mind that most IM programs tell the recipient when the other person is typing, so don't interrupt the recipient by typing while they are typing their own response.

Appropriately Conducting Multiple Conversations

- Briefly overlapping conversations are OK, but you should excuse yourself from one of the conversations if both continue beyond a few responses.
- It is totally acceptable to tell one recipient Be Right Back, or brb, if you

need to step away from the device, or are wrapping up a
second conversation.

- People speaking to you in person should take priority over the people on
IM. Under no circumstance should direct personal contact or conversations
be ignored in favor of instant messenger prompts – be polite when spoken
to and give those present in real-life your full and undivided attention.

WORK

When Instant Messaging is Appropriate

- Consider your work environment, as IM is much more appropriate in a 400-person building than a three-person office.
- Given its potential to alternately distract or facilitate faster communication in certain cases, be advised that employer policies on IM may widely differ. Determine which policies and rules of conduct apply to your workplace by talking with your supervisor or, if you are in charge, deciding what potential effect the introduction of IM would have on employees and the daily workflow.
- Note that employers may reserve the right to track, monitor and review any IM conversations made on the job.

What IM Subjects are Safe for the Workplace

- Minor details on current projects and small questions relevant to your current job or task at-hand are suitable for asking over IM. More important, sensitive or detailed questions should be made via email, in-person meetings or direct phone call.
- Work IM should not be used for jokes, questionable material, or other items not related to your job.
- Be cautious using instant messaging when contacting neighboring co-workers, as communications made this way are impersonal enough that they may get the impression that you don't want to talk to them for some reason.

Addressing Perceived Harassment Over IM

- If you believe that you are being harassed, set your IM program so that it records conversations and provide documented archives to your HR department or direct supervisor.
- Consider blocking the harassing person on IM.
- Create clear boundaries on IM by only discussing topics relevant to work.

When to Shut Instant Messengers Off

- Always set your IM program to Busy, Do Not Disturb or, better yet, shut it down entirely while conducting meetings in your office or speaking on the phone.
- When around others, keep your IM program's sound effects and audio notifications settings turned off unless you're using headphones.

- Turn off instant messaging programs whenever you leave the office for the day, even if office policy is to leave your computers on all night.

KIDS

Setting Rules for your Child's IM habits

- Start kids off slowly with instant messaging programs geared specifically towards their age group or built within online games for kids.
- Consider asking tots to use trusted, bigger-name IM clients versus lesser-known programs that may not be secure, offer unexpected (or unique and/or unusual) features, or be popular amongst shadier users.
- Teach them to use IM programs only on their own devices, and to never use or log into IM on their friend's devices.
- Make sure kids log out of all IM accounts when finished using the programs.
- If the option is offered by the software program, create a friends list on your child's IM solution so they can only chat with pre-approved parties.

Protecting Kids from Negative Chat Room Influences

- Chat rooms are more public discussion spaces than one-to-one messaging solutions, so do not allow your child to enter them until they have become comfortable with IM basics, including rules of conduct and etiquette.
- Talk to your child about the people that they meet and interact with over IM and chat room solutions, just as you would ask them about their day at school. Beyond inquiring about simple facts ("Who did you chat with?") ask them about their takeaway from the experience ("What types of things did you discuss – and how did that make you feel?").
- If necessary, set the IM client to record conversations, even though your child may feel angry about the violation of privacy.
- Tell your child to leave chat rooms immediately if he or she is not comfortable with any conversation.
- Teach children that it's OK to stick up for and defend those who make be treated unfairly or threatened – but that doing so may also make them a target.
- Create a comfortable household environment where children are encouraged to share information with you about or ask questions related to the various discussions, individuals and situations encountered online.

Sending Risky Messages

- Tell kids not to share anything over instant messengers or chat rooms that they would not share face-to-face with a stranger, including their location, phone number, or personal details.

- Your child should not share any pictures, texts, or emails that he or she isn't comfortable showing the world, even within so-called private networks – even more so, as any and all may become publicly visible.
- With children who insist on sharing risky material, it may help bring the point home to ask them what may happen if they have a falling out with the friends whom this information is being shared with.

<u>CONCLUSION</u>

There are few, if any, times in human history where technology has played such an important and overarching role in our everyday lives. Today, we're more mobile than ever, with companies suddenly selling more smartphones than PCs, and lightning-fast Internet service now available even to the most remote third world countries. At the same time, society has become more connected than ever before, with Facebook boasting nearly a billion users and political change already begun to be effected with a single tweet. In short, we have to learn how to better respect other people, and be cognizant of how our actions impact them, within this new world order.

Many of the strategies advocated here, however, can be distilled into seven basic, easily remembered points:

- Don't share personal information with strangers.
- Take active steps to safeguard children from inappropriate content or relationships.
- Clearly separate the personal from the professional world.
- Save important conversations for face-to-face talks.
- Think before you post, and consider how others will perceive what you share.
- Be fully present when you connect with others in real life.
- Speak up if you are being mistreated.

The irony: In reality, netiquette is really much the same as traditional etiquette – technology has simply become so intertwined in our everyday lives that the courtesy, thoughtfulness, and priorities we value in real life now must be applied to our virtual lives as well.

Now it's your turn. Apply the ideas, guidelines, and perspectives given here in your own life. Talk with others about how technology is changing your world, and how we as parents, professionals and digital citizens can be smarter and more responsible about integrating the best it has to offer within our day-to-day routines. Finally, recognize that rules of online and high-tech etiquette will only continue to evolve alongside the ever-growing torrent of apps, gadgets and online services. Only through continued conversation, and the participation of all sides involved, can we hope to stay ahead of the curve.

We'd be honored if you'd join us and share your discoveries, with an eye towards shaping future editions of the guide, and providing a roadmap for tomorrow's digital citizens. We invite you to reach out and join the conversation at www.AKeynoteSpeaker.com.

In the meantime, remember that technology can be fun, inspiring, and even life-changing when treated with proper dignity and respect, and as part of a well-balanced media diet. We sincerely hope that you've found this guide to be a helpful resource – and the first small step in a lifelong journey to become a better, brighter and more positive contributor to tomorrow's high-tech world.

EXPERT HINTS AND TIPS

Rich DeMuro (@RichDeMuro), Tech Reporter, KTLA-TV Los Angeles

Q: The most common breaches of high-tech etiquette you see people making and potential solutions to these problems would be?

A: The most common issues I see are people breaking the no texting or hands on phone talking while driving rules many states have set up. Not only is it really dangerous to do these things, but if I can't do it, then why should you be able to? Remember – 99.9% of emails and texts can wait.

Also, for some reason, people are still commonly sending forwards that contain false information. Before you send any "good to know" email to a bunch of friends, do a quick fact check on Snopes.com. Most of the time, your email's information was debunked years ago.

Q: Any advice for friending new people on Facebook?

A: If you're going to friend someone on Facebook, make sure you know them first! If it's someone you just met and you think you'll become friends, wait a bit before you actually friend them on Facebook unless you're certain the feeling is mutual. Everyone uses social networks differently, so try to get a feel for someone before you friend them. If they have a friends list that numbers in the thousands, they probably don't mind the random friend request. If it's in the low hundreds, they probably closely guard who they let into their circle. If it's a business thing, include a note with your request so they have a frame of reference to remember who you are.

Q: How do you de-friend someone on Facebook without causing a stir?

A: De-friending people on Facebook is a very touchy subject. No one wants to be de-friended. Even if you never talk to that person in real life, it just feels sad to get cut. Think about it this way – there must have been some reason why you friended the person in the first place. Instead of de-friending, consider adding them to Facebook's "Restricted" friends list. They will no longer be able to see much of your wall or profile and won't get any more updates from you. Then unsubscribe from their updates so you don't have to see their mugshot in your news feed. That way, it's almost like you're no longer friends but you technically still are.

Q: When is it OK to use a high-tech device (game systems, phones, etc.) in public? When should one absolutely be shut off?

A: At this point, it's becoming pretty commonplace to see gadgets just about everywhere. Our phones are our cameras and our cameras are our phones, which has opened up an entire world of possibilities. At this point, I'd go with the flow. If you see people using their devices, feel free. If there is a sign saying no phones, respect it. Otherwise, definitely keep them silent and in your pocket during movies, plays and important real-life conversations.

Q: How should you comport yourself on messaging services and text-based networks like Twitter? Any ways to avoid making huge social mistakes?

A: Twitter is a mixed bag. The good news about Twitter is that it's either public or private. There is no in-between, which frees you up when you're posting. You know your potential audience is the world. My advice is to keep your audience in mind – figure out who is following you and why, and deliver what they would expect to see from you. Everyone uses Twitter differently, so establish why you're on there and just do it.

Q: Any top tips you can share for being a better digital citizen?

A: Everyone uses the web in different ways and there is a place for everything. My best advice is to think before you do just about anything. Do you really need to make that call while eating a burger in the car? Does anyone care about your 99th check in at Starbucks? I'm not saying don't do it, but not everything has to be shared with everyone. Otherwise, just realize your strengths – be it witty commentator, early adopter or curator of cute pet pics – and go with it.

Shira Lazar, TV personality and producer and star of What's Trending

Q: What is the most common social gaffe people make with their cell phone?

A: Butt dialing, misspellings and pressing send before you're finished writing.

Q: How do you manage when technology intrudes on everyday situations – such as dates and personal one-on-one time?
A: Usually the ideal etiquette is to put your phone away on a date or other

one-on-one situation. Not on the table, but rather in your purse or pocket. Focus on the person you're with and be in the moment. If you need to check emails or texts, do it when they go to the bathroom. If there's a fun moment that you want to capture or tweet, try to restrain for future occasions. You never know if the other person even wants you to share that you're out or on a date with him/her to your entire social network, let alone how good that dessert was.

Q: What's your advice for being a better blog commenter?

A: Be quick and to the point. I'm not a big fan of being hugely negative or trolling. If you have nothing nice to say, don't say anything at all. If you want to be transparent, you can be thoughtful and honest – just be aware of the repercussions of what you say. What goes on the Internet stays there. No one likes to hear an obnoxious rant in person. If you feel that's where your comment is headed, you probably want to step away from the computer and keep it to yourself. That's what a diary is for or just happy hour with friends.

Q: How do you handle your supervisor wanting to be friends on Facebook?

A: Some people will not add anyone who works with them at all. They keep work and life very separate. I'm of the opinion that your life is online and it's out there. You might as well be authentic and take advantage of that. Not being friends with a colleague won't make too much of a difference, because everything you put online is ultimately available for anyone to see. I like adding people I work with, because it helps strengthen my relationships to them, and helps me learn more about them. Sometimes that might mean deciding not to post those select pics from that bachelorette party I went to. It's also a great way to keep in touch with work friends and colleagues once you don't work together anymore.

Christina Tynan-Wood, Author of Family Circle's Family Tech column and How to Be a Geek Goddess

Q: Essential rules as relate to modern-day high-tech, online and social networking manners include?

A: I don't really have any hard and fast rules that are different for social networking than they are for real life. If it's rude in person, it's rude online. I like manners. They were created for good reason: To help people sharing space get along better. This is why you see cultures with the smallest amount of space caring the most about manners. And I was raised by a well-mannered English woman. But I think the Internet reflects a lot of cultures, which is why it is so easy to offend. Everyone has their own idea of well-mannered.

For me, too much information is rude. So I'm offended when people share photos of intimate parts, surgeries, gross flesh wounds, etc. But some people are fascinated by this sort of thing, or there would be no reality TV. I don't think it's my business to tell other people what they should do online. But I do quietly un-friend people who share too much.

Note that un-friending is easy and best done quietly. Facebook doesn't tell people you have un-friended them so all you have to do is click that little X to get rid of them. If they are family and will notice they have been un-friended, I hide them instead.

As for friending, I like to know who I'm friending because letting people into my Facebook page gives them access to my other friends and that includes my children. But other people have their own rules about this either because they like to meet perfect strangers and are willing to take risks to do it or because they are using social media to promote a business.

Q: Your number one no-no when it comes to how users behave on social networks?

A: I don't like to tell people what to do as far as comporting yourself. In fact, I tend to silence or un-friend people who are strident and bossy online. There are a lot of different reasons for using social media and different rules apply to each. If you are just starting out at this, though, it's a good idea to stick to the basic rule (so as not to embarrass yourself): If you wouldn't stand up in front of a crowd and shout it, don't say it on Facebook or Twitter. Though some people clam up completely in front of a crowd so that rule won't really work for them.

Q: How about using high-tech devices in public – any tips you can offer there?

A: When it comes to using devices in public places, I'm pretty liberal. They are a great way to entertain yourself while alone in restaurants. Sometimes – especially if you are a parent, a doctor, or on-call for work – you really do have to take that call. But if you are socializing with people and talking to someone else on the phone, you know you are being rude. That's not to say there isn't a time when being rude isn't exactly what you want to be (i.e. your present company is hostile, an ex, or the school bully). But being rude by accident or because you are a phone addict will cost you real-world friends.

The only real "Do Not Do It!" I have (assuming you are an intelligent person capable of managing your own relationships or going without them if that is the natural consequence of your own actions) is DO NOT TEXT WHILE DRIVING. Harming your friends, passengers, and complete strangers on the road because you can't control your impulses is completely unacceptable behavior in every culture.

Stephen Balkam, CEO of the Family Online Safety Institute (FOSI)

Q: Tips you recommend for safer and more considerate social networking?

A: I'd suggest following tried and true parenting rules such as the The Golden Rule and "if you can't say something nice, don't say anything at all" – these are just as relevant online as off. Issues like cyberbullying arise because it is easier to be hurtful behind the anonymous shield of technology.

Q: Is it ever OK for parents to access their child's social network?

A: I do not believe in accessing your child's social network without their knowledge. But I do think that for emergencies and in case kids forget them, parents should know their children's passwords. I would encourage parents and kids to access social networks together at first and if they are experiencing a problem, such as an alarming or hurtful post. "Touring" sites can be very helpful at first to help everyone get acclimated to privacy settings and capabilities, which will ensure safe usage.

Q: Parents often try to monitor, restrict or intrude on kids' online/high-tech worlds – what's the appropriate etiquette here in your opinion?

A: I am a personal believer in friending your child on Facebook. I was my daughter's first Facebook friend and I think that can be very helpful. I am not her friend in order to constantly monitor her activity. Actually, I only occasionally check her activity and I do not post on her Timeline. However, by being my friend, I feel she is more thoughtful about the content she posts.

I feel that empowering your kids to be good digital citizens is more effective than parental "spying," which can anger your kids and make them feel as if you don't trust them. We should teach our kids about the appropriate use of social networks and emails before they are given an account or access.

A case could be made for checking in on younger kids' (e.g. 5 – 11 year olds) emails. As they grow, your kids should be allowed more in the way of privacy, while knowing that, from time to time, you may check in on their web history or Google their name and see what appears.

Q: Any rules of high-tech etiquette you personally have found to be most effective?

A: In our home, we try to respect the time we spend together in-person. Phones are off-limits at the dinner table. That is important family time! We have also found that setting time limits for online use is very effective. My daughter has a certain number of hours she can spend online for non-school related activities. Finally, consider using free services such as "Self-Control" which allows your child access to the web, but blocks sites you choose, such as Facebook and Twitter, while they are doing their homework.

Michael Dsupin, CEO, Talener Group

Q: A couple suggestions for appropriate blog commenting would include...?

Blog authors love comments. It validates their message or it validates that they are blogging about a point near to readers' hearts – whether you agree or disagree is irrelevant. The fact that their post hit a nerve and you chose to share your feedback matters most.

When leaving a comment, the commentator is trying to engage the author. Here are a few quick tips to make sure your blog comments are most meaningful:

• First, make sure that you use firsthand experiences and real examples to support your opinion, either pro or con.
• Second, try to be as brief as possible, yet as thorough as possible.
• Third, comment on a blog post ASAP for maximum coverage and engagement.
• Fourth, make sure you use your full name, title and company that you work for, so people can Google you and read more about your background to de-

termine your credibility level. Take for instance a restaurant recommendation that might read, "Mike says that the calamari is excellent." It's better to read that "Mike is really Mike Smith, executive chef at Per Se – thus making it a credible recommendation.

Q: When is it most appropriate to attempt to make a connection on LinkedIn?

A: Connecting with people on LinkedIn is nice to do, but not a required business practice. Therefore, I would not stop my current prospecting or business development to send an immediate LinkedIn request. I would recommend waiting until the next break, lunch or end of the day to send the request. You don't want to look too aggressive or desperate, but you do want to be timely. Don't use LinkedIn requests as a way to try to engage someone who knows that you are waiting for a response on a certain matter.

Q: What is the most common social gaffe people make with their cell phone?

A: The most social gaffe is sending an email or text before it was completed. I have hit send prematurely on countless occasions and I hate that feeling. Another one is closing lines on signatures that ask, "Please ignore any typos or spelling mistakes." Really? Do we have to ask for forgiveness? Come on man!

Marian Merritt, Norton Internet Safety Advocate, Symantec Corporation

Q: Some vital lessons that parents should teach kids when it comes to netiquette would include…?

A: Be kind online – it's just a variant of the Golden Rule… to treat others as you would have them treat you. Sometimes that is as easy to understand as not engaging in online cruelty or bullying. Other times it means don't send out links to illegal or malicious content or try to pass someone else's creation off as your own. It also means keeping your computer safe and secure so you don't send out spam or infect your network with computer viruses. Also, assume Mom (or Grandmom) will see it – anything you post, whether a video or photo or comment, can be misunderstood or be inappropriate for all audiences. Aim for G-rated content. And be ready to rewind: At some point, you will be asked to edit or remove content or remove a tag on a social media site. Be agreeable [when asked] – you might think they've overreacted, but remember what I said about being kind online…

Q: Kids and cell phones: Can they successfully mix?

A: It's important to remember that not all cell phones are smartphones. Your child may be ready for their first basic phone (e.g. one that offers just phone calls and limited texting, with no Internet or apps) when you need a way to keep in touch when you are apart. That might be if they have after-school programs or take public transportation to and from school or shuttle between family member's homes. The age at which they receive the phone may vary by child and their level of maturity.

When you decide that they do need a phone, research what your cellular provider offers in the form of discounted family plans and ability to limit phone numbers or monitor calls. Find out what your child's classmates are using. Set ground rules with your child – for example, the phone should be charged at night in a public room, never in the bedroom. Determine your budget for monthly services and how the child can reimburse you if they go over that amount. Show them how to monitor their monthly usage to avoid that problem. The phone should only be used during the times that adhere to school and household rules. And let kids know: Under what circumstances would you take the phone away? How could they earn the phone privilege back?

Parents should strive to set a good example with their own cell phone use and make sure to limit calls, texting and gaming when they are with their child. Never text or dial while driving.

A: When it comes to online etiquette and children, what foibles do kids most commonly make, and how can they avoid them?

We often think people understand our sense of humor or try to cover that with the use of emoticons. Still, people can misunderstand and take offense at a comment, a photo or even a link.

Kids (and adults) also forget how wide open the web is, unless we're actively managing to keep our privacy settings high. So they post things to present their exaggerated or idealized sense of self, often irritating or offending others in the process. Or they use what they think of as "private" or "insider" jokes, and then wonder when their parents, employers or teachers question them about it.

The anonymity of the web additionally encourages people to give vent to views that they might phrase more cautiously if they were actually in the room with the other commenters. You can see this in comments on news articles, social networks and especially throuhout political sites. Kids see this harsh online behavior from adults and believe it's acceptable.

Q: Any rules of high-tech etiquette you personally have found to be most effective in your own home?

A: With my youngest child, who is new to email, I have it setup on my smartphone so when we are out together that she can check her email. It also enables me to see at a glance who is sending her messages and if there are any problems. It helped us discuss the issue of chain letters because I saw her receive several.

With our older children, the phenomenon of people sharing their "relationship status" via social networks has been interesting. It was good to know when my son began his relationship with his girlfriend and sad when they ended it. I'm not sure he would have shared that information with me so readily otherwise, but it allowed me to understand and respect his feelings during both transitions. Of course I knew not to comment on his social network page: That would have been a parenting faux pas!

Q: Your personal rules for safe social networking would include?

A: Learn how to use privacy and security settings and talk to your friends about them. Limit how widely you share your posts. You might even think of "curating" your online self to ensure that what a stranger (such as an employer) might discover about you is all positive and safe. Many social networking sites offer you choices such as sharing items with just those you know (such as social reading apps), your close friends (in a group you create), or the general public. These varied settings can be confusing, so it's a good idea to sit down and try to figure them out, and even practice with them.

Q: Is it ever OK for parents to access their child's social network?

A: It's not OK to enter their account, either by using their phone or computer while they are logged in, unless you have explicit permission. What is OK and highly desirable is to friend your child online. You can and should talk with your child about some ground rules so you can be their friend, without embarrassing them or yourself. Most parents quickly learn that they shouldn't publicly comment on their child's posts (but you can always send a private message about it). Not all kids are bothered by sharing their social space with their parents, but respect each other's privacy if you can.

Q: What's appropriate etiquette as far as parents' monitoring kids' online habits is concerned?

A: Monitoring is a great parenting approach, especially with younger children. You should always talk with your child before installing or using parental control or monitoring tools though, setting guidelines for what you will see and what your household rules are. You should also aspire to give your child greater online freedom as they get older and as they demonstrate that they are capable of staying safe.

I believe a parent should absolutely check the email of a younger child. Email can contain spam and spam can be both adult in nature and dangerous. You need time to coach your child to recognize what is safe and what is suspicious and how to handle the latter. Set up "white lists" of safe senders and show your child how to block unwanted messages. As the child gets older, you should only check in from time to time to ensure they are continuing to manage email well. Ask your child to login and sit together and discuss what you find. If you don't recognize senders, ask your child to identify them. You may find that your child has signed up for services you were unaware of or participating in chain letters.

Amelia McDonell-Parry, Editor-in-Chief, TheFrisky.com

Q: At what point during a relationship is it OK to update your Facebook status, if ever?
A: Personally, I haven't done it since I was engaged and then my fiancée dumped me, and I had to deal with the instantaneous "Oh nooooooooos" that flooded my wall the second I changed my status to "single" again. And I don't think I will ever have my status list ANYTHING unless, maybe, I'm married. But for everyone else – now that I've presented the worst case

scenario – you really shouldn't change your status until you've discussed your real-life status with your significant other. It's kind of psycho to change your status to "In A Relationship" and the guy you've been going out with for three weeks sees it and is, like, "Oh, news to me."

Q: Just how bad is it to break up with someone over a text, email or instant messenger communication?

A: To a certain degree the severity of each really depends on how long you've been together, but regardless, I think all of the above are insanely rude, so...

Text – A 10 on a scale of 1 to 10, because you can't even really write anything of substance in one!

Email – It's a 7, because at least the person doing the breaking up can go on and on about how it's them and not you.

IM – I'd give it an 8, but at least it gives the one being dumped a chance to respond. But seriously, IM... how 1995! I mean, you don't even use Skype now?

Q: What are the rules of technology, as relates to dating?

A: Keep your phone on silent and face down on the table if you HAVE to have it out. And then check to see whether you've gotten any calls or texts when one of you goes to the bathroom. I did this last night, as I texted with a friend about how boring my date was and how I would rather talk to the guy playing gypsy guitar at the front of the bar.

Judith Kallos, Creator, NetManners.com

Q: What should you do if you boss wants to be friends on Facebook?

A: Politely let them know that you appreciate your personal privacy being respected and that you do not "friend" those who you have a strictly professional relationship with. Now, if you are really friends in the true sense of the word, you wouldn't ask that question, right?

Q: Is it appropriate to automatically follow people on Twitter?

124

A: Not unless you are truly interested in what they have to say....

Q: Is there an appropriate way to respect them and not follow them back?

A: Following has nothing to do with respect. Because someone you don't know (or even possibly do) follows you does not mean that you have an obligation to follow them back. It's the same with friending. Chances are they won't even notice if you do or not anyway. ☺

Jeana Lee Tahnk, Tech PR and Marketing Specialist

Q: Is it ever appropriate to reach out to potential clients through unusual channels like social networks or their personal blogs?

A: Yes, as long as you're reaching out in a tactful and professional way. But take the hint if you haven't received a response after one or two messages and realize that they're probably not interested, at least for now.

Q: Is there an eloquent way to de-friend someone on Facebook?
The way that Facebook is setup, you can de-friend someone without them knowing. If you prefer to keep them in your network, you can simply make someone an "Acquaintance" and see fewer status updates from them. If you're ready to cut the online tie altogether and de-friend, and then are confronted about it, you can simply say that you were cleaning up your contacts and wanted to limit your social network to the people you most regularly communicate with.

Q: Is it ever OK for parents to access their child's social network, e.g. Facebook?

A: Facebook monitoring for kids, especially those who are underage, is of utmost importance. There are many ways in which to monitor kids, and parents' secretly logging into their kids' Facebook accounts is one way that parents are doing it. In an ideal world, however, the lines of communication are open much wider and parents don't need to sneak around to know what their kids' online activity is. There are great tools to help parents with the monitoring process – MinorMonitor is one of them that enables them to track keywords and suspicious friends. The best thing to do is start the conversation early and make it a collaboration rather than a conspiracy. If your kids are going to start enjoying an online presence, make sure they know that you'll be there every step of the way.

Tim Stevens, Editor-in-Chief, Engadget

Q: What is the most common social flub that people make when it comes to using mobile devices and cell phones?

A: Far and away the most common social gaffe people make with their phones is pulling them out in the middle of small social gatherings, say, dinner out with a loved one. This is definitely increasing in terms of social acceptance, but it's still rude to whip out your smartphone while someone is talking to you. It's always best to wait for them to take their phone out first or, if you must peek, at least wait for the conversation to die down.
Far less common but far more annoying is a phone ringing during a movie. There's a reason that the pre-show trailers remind you three times to silence your phones. Don't be that guy or gal who needs a fourth reminder!

Q: Is there an elegant, unobtrusive way to get rid of unwanted Facebook friends?

A: There is no really easy and graceful way to do it, unfortunately. A lot of people post an update saying "Sorry, I need to prune my friends list, it's nothing personal." But that's just the equivalent of saying that "I have friends I like more than you." The best you can do is move someone to a list that sees none of your status updates and has limited access to your info on there. That way you're still "friends" but they aren't seeing your every move.

Q: How can people be more productive commenters on blogs, newsgroups and other public forums?

A: The best way to be a good commenter is to relax! People get incredibly uptight, defensive and offensive. Nobody likes a troll, even other trolls, and if you find yourself getting into fights in comments sections constantly, chances are you need to get out from under that bridge!

ABOUT THE AUTHORS

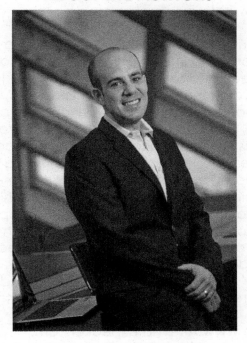

SCOTT STEINBERG
KEYNOTE SPEAKER | STRATEGIC CONSULTANT |
BESTSELLING AUTHOR | FUTURIST
www.AKeynoteSpeaker.com

Scott Steinberg is one of the world's best-known business strategists and strategic innovation consultants, and the CEO of TechSavvy Global, a management consulting and market research firm which helps clients create value and cultivate competitive advantage on the back of emerging innovations and trends. A strategic advisor to Fortune 500 firms, non-profits, schools and startups, he aids partners with identifying emerging opportunities and developing powerful leadership, marketing and content strategies designed to capitalize on rising business, social and technology trends.

Among today's most-quoted keynote speakers and technology analysts, he's consulted on dozens of market-leading products and services, and authored nine books including international best sellers The Crowdfunding Bible and The Modern Parent's Guide, and the critically-acclaimed Business Expert's Guidebook. His motivational speeches, leadership seminars and training workshops show executives and educators how to become more effective – and make both they and their businesses indispensable in an increasingly disposable world.

As an industry consultant, Steinberg has helped top corporations from Microsoft, Sony and Intel to ESPN and MTV adapt to changing consumer, high-tech and social trends. Hailed as a top technology futurist by leading media outlets including NPR, BusinessWeek and The Wall St. Journal, his advisory work enables clients to identify emerging cultural and technological forces and create powerful business strategies that meet changing market needs.
This eye for business analysis has led to his work as a strategic insider for 600+ publications from CNN to The New York Times and Fast Company, and pioneer in the field of digital publishing. A nationally-syndicated columnist who routinely explores topics including change, innovation and connecting generations, he's also the creator and host of Gear Up, Rolling Stone's first dedicated blog and video series devoted to consumer technology. A regular guest on ABC, CBS, FOX and NBC, he serves as a featured expert for Fast Company, VentureBeat, The Huffington Post and more.

For more info, see www.AKeynoteSpeaker.com.

Damon Brown covers tech culture for Playboy and Family Circle, and is the author of several books including Barnes & Noble's NOOK: The Official Guide and the critically-acclaimed Porn & Pong: How Grand Theft Auto, Tomb Raider and Other Sexy Games Changed Our Culture. His newest book is Damon Brown's Simple Guide to Twitter, the latest in his best-selling Simple Guide series. Visit him at www.damonbrown.net and follow him on Twitter at www.twitter.com/browndamon.

ADDITIONAL RESOURCES

❝ Unbelievably packed with practical, useful and valuable advice.❞
—John Jantsch, Author, *Duct Tape Marketing*

THE
BUSINESS
EXPERT'S
GUIDEBOOK

- ☑ Small Business Tips
- ☑ Technology Trends
- ☑ Online Marketing

SCOTT STEINBERG

Foreword by **Scott Gerber**, Founder, Young Entrepreneur Council

HOW TO: LAUNCH ANY STARTUP + WIN WITH SOCIAL MEDIA + TURBOCHARGE SALES

Download FREE Now

www.AKeynoteSpeaker.com

> **Don't start a crowdfunding campaign without it!**
> – Brian Fargo, Creator, *Wasteland 2*

THE
Crowdfunding
B I B L E

HOW TO RAISE MONEY FOR ANY
STARTUP, VIDEO GAME, OR PROJECT

By
SCOTT STEINBERG

with **RUSEL DeMARIA**

Edited by JON KIMMICH

Foreword by **ERIC MIGICOVSKY**, Creator, Pebble: E-Paper Watch

Download FREE Now

www.AKeynoteSpeaker.com

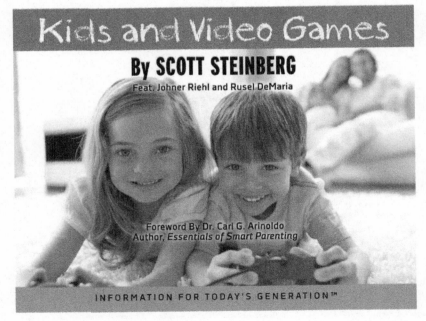

ALSO AVAILABLE:

CPSIA information can be obtained
at www.ICGtesting.com
Printed in the USA
LVOW03s1345180817
545347LV00001B/137/P